Scottish Football Heroes

BILLY BREMNER'S

Scottish Football Heroes

The Breedon Books
Publishing Company
Derby

First published in Great Britain by
The Breedon Books Publishing Company Limited
Breedon House, 44 Friar Gate, Derby, DE1 1DA.
1997

ISBN 1 85983 077 3

Printed and bound by Butler & Tanner Ltd., Selwood Printing
Works, Caxton Road, Frome, Somerset.

Colour separations by RPS, Leicester.

Jackets printed by Lawrence-Allen, Weston-super-Mare, Avon.

To Jimmy

with best wishes

from Roy & Sheena

aug 1997.

Contents

Foreword

ONE of my personal football heroes is Billy Bremner. Who can ever forget him in those distinctive white colours of Leeds United or, even better, in the famous blue shirt of Scotland. He was every manager's dream midfielder, or wing-half as we used to call them in those days.

Billy was a fantastic player and when one of your own heroes talks about his heroes, then you know it is time to listen.

His book, Scotland's Soccer Heroes, is a great reminder of the wealth of football talent that has been naturally produced in that country over the decades.

Hopefully, this reminder of Scottish soccer at its best will not only jog the memories but will inspire today's youngsters to work hard at their game and provide us with the heroes of tomorrow, young men who will bring honour to Scotland in every corner of the world.

Football is the greatest game on earth and Scotland has produced some of its greatest players, its major stars. And nobody is more qualified to talk about them than Billy Bremner — after all, he is one of the greatest of those stars.

CRAIG BROWN

My Story

HEROES!... We all have them — screen stars, super sports stars, even politicians. In my case, just like millions of others, my heroes kicked a ball about on a Saturday afternoon. I had my heroes as a boy and I still have my heroes today — even though I can still be stopped as I walk down the street and asked for an autograph myself.

I can't really remember how or when soccer first entered my life. It seems to me that it has always been there. As long ago as I can remember wearing shoes I can remember having a football to kick. I took a keen interest in the game as a spectator, too, and grew up as a Celtic supporter. I never got into the religious divide, however, and felt quite comfortable going to see Rangers — or any other club come to that! I was a Celtic supporter simply because they were my chosen team.

At primary school I was in the school team and that trend continued when I went on to St Modwen's High School. I was football daft. I listened to the radio all the time to pick up all the information that I could, and I read every magazine and newspaper that I could lay my hands on. At the same time I was selected to play for my county side and then, eventually,

I was picked for Scotland schoolboys. I made my very first appearance at Wembley with the schoolboys team. It was in 1958 and I remember that Terry Venables was in the England line-up.

Just to keep the record straight, there was another team that I followed avidly — even though I've already told you that I was a Celtic supporter. As a boy I was always fascinated by the name of this club. I know that it also works in reverse in that I have met people who followed teams like Albion Rovers, Partick Thistle or Queen of the South, simply because they were attracted by the name. Some people even back horses on the same basis! Well, my dream team from afar, so to speak, was Exeter City. I didn't have the slightest clue where they were. All I knew was that they had a great name and, because of that, they must be a great team to play for.

You can see how my mind worked. I was already thinking about who I might like to play for as a professional. It never occurred to me that I might not make the grade. All I thought about was following in the footsteps of my footballing heroes — players like Bobby Collins and George Young.

Of course, wanting a career in soccer and actually getting one are two quite different things. Many eager lads have been heartbroken after being rejected by clubs, and I'm sure that a lot of talent has gone to waste because clubs did not recognise the latent potential that was right under their noses. I was one of the lucky ones. On the strength of my schoolboy international appearances, there were a number of clubs which showed an interest in me. I became pals with a lad called Tommy Henderson, and we both seemed to be in demand.

I did a week's trial with Arsenal and another with Chelsea. Sheffield Wednesday were interested in me, as were Aston Villa. I was in no hurry to make a commitment, though. The truth is that I really wanted to join Celtic and I was hoping that they too might show an interest in me. My father had other ideas however. He had no intention of allowing me to get caught up in any religious kick.

"You're going to England and that's that!" he said.

The next thing that I knew was that, through some family connection, I was approached by Harry Vennals, a director of Leeds United. He was a very impressive man ...typical of the Bulldog Breed, with short-cropped hair, thick neck and clipped speech. But he had a kindly eye.

I had never even considered Leeds among my possible clubs, for the very good reason that I had hardly heard of them. I knew about John Charles of course — but I knew nothing about his club, Leeds United. Bill Lambton was manager at that time, and I didn't know much about him either. It helped that my pal Tommy Henderson was also being offered a place at Elland Road, and so I agreed to give it a go.

I'd like to be able to tell you that I had a wonderful time from day one, but that was not so. The truth is that I was very unhappy. It wasn't just me either — Tommy was fed-up as well. We were both very homesick and we did not see much hope for the future. When we joined the club, Leeds had more than 50 professionals and ran four teams. You were lucky to get anywhere near a game in the reserves.

There we were — two 15-year-olds with ambition. We resolved that if we did not get into the Central League side by the end of the season, then we would leave and go back to Scotland. Our resolution certainly made us feel better. As it happened, I did get into the reserves — a rare thing for someone of my age. Tommy was true to his word. He didn't make it to the club's second string and went home. Later he joined Celtic and Hearts. Ironically, he returned to Leeds some years later when he was bought by Don Revie.

As for me, life went on but, although I did make progress at Leeds, I could not find a cure for my homesickness. When I made my League debut for Leeds against Chelsea at Stamford Bridge in 1960, I was far from happy. In fact I was downright miserable, even though I'd played my part in a 3-1 win. Despite being given such a golden opportunity, I was still pining to get back to my native Scotland. I was only 17 at the time and, really, I wasn't yet old enough to know my own mind. Several times I came really close to getting on the next train back to Stirling. Relegation for the club at the end of my first season in the senior team didn't help.

For about three years my attitude stayed the same. I wanted away ...back across the border to what I thought would be happiness.

On the eve of my first-team debut for Leeds, my room-mate in the London hotel was an experienced inside-right. Someone of whom you may have heard. His name was Don Revie. I was on the right wing in those days and Don helped me a lot during the game. He also helped me a lot when we were off the pitch.

Spending time with him made me realise what a deep thinker he was, and I knew that he would make his mark when he became a manager. In those early days I used to do a bit of baby-sitting for Don and his wife, Elsie. In a sense, as his children grew up, so did Leeds ...and me along with them.

Much happened when I was 19. I was still homesick and, even after my marriage to Vicky, I still could not get used to life in England. I wasn't lonely any more but I was still unable to settle. I asked for a transfer more than once and even Don Revie, who had replaced Jack Taylor in March 1961, as player-manager, began to get impatient and one day sent for me in his office. He wanted to know where he and the club stood in my plans for the future.

"It's no good keeping on like this. You must make up your mind whether you're going to be a Leeds United player or move on," he said, quite forcefully.

It brought me to my senses a bit and I resolved to stay. And the moment I had made the commitment, my homesickness evaporated. Everything seemed to fall into place. I knew that I could enjoy life at Leeds and that Scotland was not so very far away ...that I could quite easily slip home for a few days here and there. I no longer felt trapped and a prisoner away from my beloved country.

Word about me being unsettled had reached the ears of Walter Galbraith, who was with Hibernian. He asked me direct how much Leeds would want for me. It was not the sort of question that I felt I could answer. In the end, Hibs put in a bid of £25,000. I wandered around totally confused. I had just made my mind up that I was staying but then, when a serious offer came in from a Scottish club, I couldn't help being thrilled at the possibility.

At the time, Leeds United were not in good shape. Relegation from the old First Division, and a dangerous flirtation with relegation to the Third Division, had both taken their toll. The club had fallen into debts of more than £200,000 — which was a great deal of money in those days. However, Revie was intent on a rebuilding programme and was not at all keen to sell. He responded to the Hibs offer by pushing up the price to £30,000. Everton also came in with a bid of £25,000, but Revie threatened to resign if the board sold me. The new price was too much for Hibernian and the whole idea of a move was dropped. I was later told by Les Cocker, one of our coaches at that time, that Revie never had any intention of selling me and would have simply kept on increasing the price until the subject was dropped.

There was another bonus in store for me. Not only did I sign a new long-term contract with Leeds, but Revie bought a new player to captain the side. It was in March 1962 that he crossed the Pennines to sign my hero, Bobby Collins, from Everton for £25,000. Just imagine! — I was going to play in the same side as the great Bobby Collins. He was 31 at that time, and many critics said that wee Bobby was finished — over the hill. Don Revie answered them by saying: "I've bought an experienced general to organise my young players!"

Well, that tremendous little Scot did organise Revie's troops and soon had us marching on to glory. Following his arrival, Leeds began to climb steadily up and up. In 1962-63 we just missed promotion finishing fifth. The following season we were Second Division champions with Sunderland as runners-up. It seems like only yesterday that we played that title-clinching match at Swansea. Alan Peacock scored twice and Johnny Giles hit one to put us — and keep us — in the driving seat.

In the dressing-room after the game the champagne flowed as we congratulated each other on our first real achievement together. So, we were back in the First Division and, although I had always believed that one day Leeds would be a great side, I hardly dreamed of the heights to which we would eventually aspire, or that I — a player who had not made it easy for Don Revie — would also lead them as skipper.

From the time that we were promoted back into the First Division, Leeds United never looked back. Of course, we had our disappointments, but for me they were character building. We came desperately close to doing the double in 1965. We finished as runners-up to Manchester United in the League — level on points, but slightly inferior in the goals department. We also reached the FA Cup Final, but lost 2-1 to Liverpool — after extra time!

For me, these were thrilling and memorable times, tinged with tears of disappointment which only added to our determination. I'm a typical Scot! I hate losing! That doesn't mean that I'm a bad loser — but I do hate it. All my heroes basked in glory and I wanted to do the same. You never hear about their bad performances or their defeats so, when you are trying to follow in their footsteps and then you get a setback, it really hurts.

There is one great pain-killer for disappointment — it's called success. At Leeds we were not allowed to feel sorry for ourselves for long because there was so much to get on with. Over the years there has been a great myth built up about Don Revie and his version of Leeds United. We have been called robots, ruthless, assassins, spoilers and much worse. Nothing could be further from the truth.

I can honestly say that if we were hard at times it was simply because of individual expression. We were never coached or directed to be hard — but we did have this great personal motivation to be first to the ball, and to win. We were hard but fair at all times, and I doubt that we gave anything like as much as we were expected to take.

As for being defensive, robotic, a machine — or any other of the labels that people attempted to pin on us — what complete and utter rubbish! We were a team of enthusiastic, skilful professional footballers who were all on the same wavelength and therefore played as a complete unit. After all — and correct me if I'm wrong — isn't football meant to be a team game?

Don Revie left us to sort ourselves out during a game. Our preparations were never about endless set-pieces, or long discussions about tactics. We would talk about the opposition — their style, their weaknesses and that sort of thing — hardly ever about ourselves. I can remember Revie once having a go at us and saying: "Don't keep looking to me on the bench to find out what to do. You're playing the game — so play it!"

Does that sound like a man who expected his players to follow his instructions like clockwork soldiers?

Getting back to success at Leeds — when Revie called me into his office one day and told me that he wanted me to be captain, I couldn't wait to phone home and tell everyone. It wasn't just that I was taking over the captaincy from my hero Bobby Collins, but I felt that I was bringing further honour to my family and to Scotland.

We had become a team to be feared and respected — but

we had still not actually won anything. That is until the 1967-68 season when things changed with a vengeance and we landed both the League Cup and the European Fairs Cup — which is now known as the UEFA Cup of course.

The League Cup Final at Wembley saw us facing Arsenal. We beat them 1-0 in a game which some critics described as one of the worst at Wembley. How often have we heard that? It was said to be a game dominated by defence — and perhaps that is right as it took a defender, Terry Cooper, to score the goal which clinched the trophy. After so many disappointments, lifting that League Cup and showing it to our supporters at Wembley was a marvellous magic moment that I shall never forget.

There was still more to come just a few weeks later. In the 1967 Final of the Fairs Cup we had been beaten by Dynamo Zagreb with a 2-0 aggregate in their favour. It taught us a lesson and, by beating Hibs, Rangers and Dundee United in a rare sequence of matches, we reached the 1968 Final to face Ferencvaros of Hungary.

The first leg was at Elland Road, and a Mick Jones goal gave us the advantage for the second leg. We were confident because we thought that our defence could handle whatever the Hungarians had to offer. Our confidence proved to be well-founded because the return leg in Budapest ended in a 0-0 draw — giving us an aggregate 1-0 victory.

Our first victory in Europe was celebrated in our hotel, along with Lord Harewood, president of Leeds, and his two sons, who were in the party. As the evening went on into the early hours we began a sing-song and I was delegated to act as compere and to conduct the proceedings. Everyone present —

players, Don Revie, members of the press, even Lord Harewood, had to take it in turn to sing a song. I'm not going to reveal exactly what the earl sang — but it brought the house down.

At long last, after being known as the best runners-up in the game, we had two pots on the sideboard in the boardroom at Elland Road. Those successes were great — but it was the big one we wanted — the League title.

The following season we made our exit from the Fairs Cup at the hands of Ujpest Dozsa, after having already defeated Standard Liege, Napoli and Hanover. We were also out of the FA Cup and the League Cup — so it had to be the League championship or nothing. Throughout the season we had managed to keep our noses in front at the top of the First Division and, toward the end, only one team — Liverpool — stood much chance of overhauling us. We had to play them at Anfield, aware that one point in the Liverpool fortress would give us the title.

Nearly 54,000 packed into Anfield for the duel of the giants, and thousands more were locked outside. The action was furious as both sides gave their all in a battle which meant so much to both teams. We got our point in a game which was certainly not short of thrills and incidents.

When it was all over there came one of the most moving moments of my life. As we did a lap of honour, the Kop took us to their hearts and cheered us — the new champions — as if we were their own side.

During my 17 years at Elland Road, which include more than 770 first-team games, there were many great experiences. There were the disappointments of being so near and yet so far when we were beaten Finalists or championship run-ners-up. But there were also the two League titles, two European Fairs victories, the League Cup win, the FA Charity Shield win — and there was the moment every footballer dreams of yet so few ever realise — winning the FA Cup.

My moment for that particular dream coming true was on 6 May 1972. Our old friends Arsenal were, once again, at the opposite end. It was another hard-fought game in which defences held the key to success. On the day, our defences proved to be water-tight while Arsenal's sprung just the smallest of leaks — allowing Allan Clarke to score one of the most important goals of his career. At the final whistle, Arsenal hung their heads in disbelief. We had done it again — beaten them 1-0.

After those heady days at Elland Road, I was transferred to Hull City in September 1976 for £25,000, and I remained at Boothferry Park until I officially retired in May 1978. I did actually play a few more games after I became manager at Doncaster Rovers in November 1978. We were very short of players and so I turned out four times in emergencies.

I remained as manager of Doncaster Rovers until 1985 and we were twice promoted from Division Four. Then, in Octo-ber 1985, my pal Eddie Gray left his job as manager of Leeds and I was asked to take over. I had been quite happy at Don-caster but the chance to follow in the footsteps of Don Revie at Leeds was too tempting by far. I took up the challenge. Sadly, the club was not in good shape. There was nothing to spend, and the possibility of getting Leeds out of the, then, Second Division seemed very remote.

On 28 September 1988, I left the club. It was a sad

moment but probably the best thing for all concerned. I became a 'media expert' for the rest of the season and then, at the end of June 1989, I was approached by Doncaster again. They had just parted company with Joe Kinnear who had been manager there for only three months, Dave Mackay having been in charge there before him.

I remained at Doncaster for two years before deciding that I had had enough and resigned in November 1991. Since then I have resisted various temptations to go back into management. It is a thankless task and should carry a government health warning.

Today, I still live within easy reach of Leeds, Hull and Doncaster, the three clubs which have featured in my career in English soccer. I am still called upon to take part in television, radio and newspaper match coverage, as well as being kept busy attending football functions all over the world.

My house is full of soccer awards and mementoes, including my much-treasured Footballer of the Year award for the 1969-70 season. Some say that I would have won it much earlier if I had learned to keep my mouth shut. I realise that my explosive temperament, during the heat of the moment on the field of play, did not exactly enhance my chances in previous seasons. That's the price I had to pay for being the fiery, red-blooded, red-headed Scot that I am.

I did learn to curb my tongue and my temper, but I was never able to change the fact that I was — and still am — a passionate Scotsman. Although my soccer career has chiefly taken place in England, my heart has always remained in Scotland — which is why I was so very proud and thrilled every time I was asked to pull on the famous dark blue shirt of my country.

I was drafted into the Scotland squad by Jock Stein and I remember travelling to Poland and Finland with them as Scotland tried to qualify for the 1966 World Cup in England. Those trips were part of my education although I was a little frustrated at not being selected to play.

One day Jock pulled me to one side and told me: "You won't be long before you are in the side. These are important qualifying matches and we need the experienced international players. Your time will come — and it will come soon."

Eventually, of course, my time did come. My first cap was against Spain at Hampden Park on 8 May 1965. When the team was announced and I knew that I was playing you could not get me away from the telephone — I just had to tell everyone. It was a proud wee Scotsman who walked out at Hampden for his first full cap.

The Hall of Fame is a room set aside in the Scottish Football Association headquarters in Glasgow. Scotsmen who have won 50 or more caps have their portraits hung there and I am immensely proud to say that I am among those who have represented their country on a sufficient number of occasions to warrant a place in that wonderful place.

Oddly enough, my first cap was a 0-0 draw, and my 50th cap, similarly, was a 0-0 draw — when we met Brazil in Frankfurt in the 1974 World Cup finals. I also had the honour of being captain of Scotland for several seasons and one of our most memorable results was a 2-1 win over Zaire in that same 1974 World Cup tournament. It was memorable because it was our first-ever victory in a World Cup finals match.

In all I won 54 senior caps for Scotland, my last being in 1975 in a 3-1 win over Denmark at Hampden Park in a European Championship qualifier. Unfortunately it was not enough for us to make it to the finals of 1976 and, as Scotland's hopes ended, so did my international career.

I do not go to the Scottish FA headquarters to gaze at my picture. Despite my on-the-pitch image I am quite a shy person really but, if my career has inspired even one young player to take his footballing career seriously — and to perhaps look forward to enjoying the same sort of success that has meant so much to me — then that is reward enough for me.

As I said at the beginning, we all need our heroes — our inspirations — and in the following pages I have selected, what I believe to be, some of the most talented Scotsmen ever to have pulled on football boots.

In today's game the heroes have become of pop-star status. The facilities for playing the game at the highest level would rank five stars in an hotel guide, and football itself has taken on a new look with a much lighter ball, boots that resemble carpet-slippers, umpteen substitutes on the bench, such new positions as wing-back, striker and central defender — plus saturation coverage by the media that yields millions of pounds in revenue.

All these changes …and yet the game of football remains essentially the same as it has always been — a number of young men kicking a ball about with a will to win, a passion to play …and a desire to emulate their heroes.

For Scotsmen, that will, that passion, and that desire is

more vibrant than for most. The skirl of the pipes and the breeze on the heather is embodied in the hearts of all true Scots — as is the sound of boot against ball, ball against net, and the roar of a crowd showing its approval. It's the stuff that creates football heroes and there are none that are greater than Scottish Soccer Heroes.

The Lawman

WHEN he was a lad, sitting on the train heading for England, nobody else in the same carriage would have given him a second glance. Today, 20 years after his retirement, Denis Law remains one of the most popular footballing stars ever to come out of Scotland.

Denis did not exactly look the part when he arrived at Huddersfield station to begin a career that was to take him to far more exotic locations, as he himself explained when recalling that moment when he stepped down off the train.

"It was Bill Shankly, if my memory serves me correctly, who came down to the railway station to meet me. What a shock it must have been for him when he first set eyes on me.

"There I stood, bag in one hand, ticket in the other, a slim — that's putting it politely — lad. A strange youngster in strange surroundings and, to cap it all, sporting a pair of steel-rimmed spectacles. I don't know exactly what Bill Shankly's feelings must have been. I seem to remember him casting his eyes desperately up and down the platform, as if unable to believe that this apparition was really the lad who had travelled all the way down from Aberdeen to join his club on the strong recommendation of their Scottish section."

That was a pretty fair assessment. Shankly was actually far less polite in his own account of that meeting. He described Law as looking like a 'plucked chicken'. However, the then assistant Huddersfield boss was able to recognise a potential star when he saw one. He arranged an eye operation for Law and ordered a change of diet, which ensured plenty of steak, Denis developed, made the first team and never looked back.

The Denis Law Story is quite remarkable. He was born in Aberdeen on 24 February 1940, the youngest of seven children. His father was a trawlerman and, but for his rare footballing talent, Denis would also have been heading for a life on the ocean wave.

Before he was 14, Denis had never even worn a pair of real football boots. Nevertheless, his talent was spotted and he made it to the Aberdeen district's under-15 side and that is where he was discovered by Archie Beattie, brother of Andy who was manager of Huddersfield. The problem with Law's sight was a squint which meant that he could hardly see out of one eye.

When he joined Huddersfield he was immediately put on the ground-staff — which meant cleaning the dressing-rooms, sweeping the terraces, and training. He was paid £5 per week for this and, like me, he became very, very homesick. Also like me, Denis made progress very quickly. It was April 1955 when he joined Huddersfield and he was not much more than 15 years old. On 24 December 1956 he made his League debut at Meadow Lane in a 2-1 win over Notts County. Just two days later he made his home debut in the Christmastime return match with the Magpies. This time Huddersfield won 3-1 and Denis scored his first-ever League goal. A star had been born and he had not even signed professional forms yet!

On 18 October 1958, Denis was awarded his first senior cap for Scotland. Matt Busby was in charge of the Scotland squad and he saw the potential dynamite in Law's slight frame. At 18 years, 7 months and 24 days, Denis became the youngest senior Scotland player this century. Scotland were playing Wales in Cardiff and won 3-0 and, as you might expect, Denis celebrated in style by scoring on his debut.

His career had got off to a sensational start and, as his reputation preceded him, Denis found himself the subject of tight marking and tough tackles. He responded in kind, of course, and was then given the 'fiery Scot' label that so many of us apparently earned when we demonstrated that we didn't actually like having lumps kicked out of us.

Denis has always been passionate about his football and his enthusiasm is still very evident today when you hear him commenting on radio or television. He once admitted, however, to being the worst possible football fan.

"I wouldn't have taken a twopenny bus ride to watch a football match," said Denis. "Come to think of it, I wouldn't even have been tempted if someone had sent a chauffeur-driven limousine to take me to Old Trafford. I was only ever interested in playing — I couldn't stand to watch the game. If I wasn't playing, you'd find me baby-sitting, washing up, or anything rather than sitting down to watch a game of soccer.

"I used to get either bored or frustrated by simply watching, and that is what put me off. Gradually, though, I became a convert and started to see football in a different light. It is possible to watch it as a fan rather than as a player and, whereas at one time I thought that once I had hung up my boots that would be an end of it, I find that now I get a lot of pleasure from going to watch as many games as possible."

It was 1974 before Denis finally called it a day. His career was like his play — sensational! In 1960, Manchester City smashed the British transfer record by paying £55,000 to sign him from Huddersfield. He had certainly made his mark in Yorkshire with 16 goals in 81 League games. Yet that was merely the start. In a year at Maine Road he hit 21 goals in 44 games and that started the pilgrims from Italy beginning journeys to Manchester to see him in action.

City were far from keen to sell him but the temptation of doubling their money became too great and, after little more than a year at Maine Road, the Lawman was on his way to Torino for £110,000 — an unheard of amount in those days.

If Denis had been homesick when he first joined Huddersfield it was as nothing compared to his Torino torment. He has said that it was the unhappiest time of his life and I, for one, believe him. I have never been tempted to go abroad to play, other than as a visitor for international or European games.

"It was like a prison," said Denis. "It wasn't long before I realised that I had made a big mistake. I only wanted to be treated like a human being but that seemed to be asking too much. It appeared that the club felt that it wasn't just your services that they had bought for a while, but that they owned you body and soul. You were there to do their bidding day and night. I hated it — especially when Torino refused to give me leave to play for Scotland.

News of Law's unhappiness soon spread to England, and there a fellow Scot who had already had first-hand experience of his skills, planned a rescue package. Matt Busby put in a bid of £115,000, and that was good enough to convince Torino to release Law to Manchester United. In 27 games for Torino, Law had scored 10 goals. Not a bad record and there were mixed feelings among the Italian fans when he was allowed to leave. There were no such feelings at Old Trafford. The supporters were well aware that Busby would not have broken the British transfer record for nothing and they extended a warm welcome to the player who, little more than a year earlier, had been one of the enemy at Maine Road.

It was 12 July 1962 when Law signed for Manchester United and he remained at Old Trafford for almost 11 years. During that time he became the undisputed 'Goal King' of British soccer — and certainly the No.1 hero of the United fans. It was not completely a bed of roses for Denis, however. His temperament did, occasionally, get him into trouble — and the ensuing suspensions always earned quite a ticking-off from Matt Busby. There was another time, too, when the two men did not see quite eye to eye. It was in 1966 at a time when Denis felt that he was due for a better deal and threatened to quit if he didn't get one. Busby immediately met the challenge by putting him on the transfer list. Just a few days later, Denis was man enough to make a public apology.

These were quite isolated incidents. For the greater part, Denis had a fantastic time with Manchester United. In 1964 he was named European Footballer of the Year, an honour which no other Scot has yet managed to achieve. He twice won League championship medals and, in 1963, he realised a personal dream when he scored in the FA Cup Final at Wembley in which United beat Leicester 3-1.

Denis loved the cut and thrust of cup football. In the FA Cup he scored 34 goals in 44 matches — at that time a record. He set up another record when he hit 28 goals in 33 games in European competition. Despite all this, he was unable to take part in United's most memorable night. A knee injury forced Denis to miss the 1968 European Cup Final in which his club beat Benfica. He had played a major part in the European campaign but, at the last moment, was forced out of the moment of glory.

Irony was never lost on Denis. When he was with Manchester City in 1961, he once hit six goals in an FA Cup tie against Luton, only for the game to be abandoned and the slate wiped clean. The Lawman took all this in his stride and just laughed it off. He knew that there were more golden goals to come from his feet of dynamite.

There was a final irony to his League career when United gave him a free transfer in July 1973. Denis had been plagued by a knee injury for two years and, as a gesture, United made him a free agent in order that he could either retire gracefully or negotiate a new deal elsewhere. He chose to battle on and joined Manchester City for the second time. In April 1974 he scored in the end-of-season derby game with United. It was a simple back-heel into the net, but this time there was no salute of celebration from the Lawman. He knew that he had just scored the goal that would guarantee relegation for his old club and the thought prevented him from having any feeling of celebration.

His United career had yielded 171 goals in 309 League appearances — plus, of course, all those wonderful Cup goals both at home and in Europe. During that final season with City he added a further nine goals in 24 League games — and still he was not quite finished.

If Denis Law was a legend in English League football, he was also a remarkable servant for his country. After his first senior appearance for Scotland in 1958, he went on to win a total of 55 caps — the last of which came in the 1974 World Cup finals in Germany. Willie Ormond was manager of Scotland and he ignored the fact that Denis was now 34 years old and had a dodgy knee.

"There was no way I could let Denis finish his career without ever appearing in the World Cup finals," said Willie.

I had the honour of being captain of that Scotland squad and we only narrowly — very narrowly — failed to get past our group matches. We were the first team ever to go out of the World Cup finals on goal difference alone. If we had scored just one more goal we would probably have gone through to the next round and it would have been Brazil on the next plane home.

As it was, Denis ended his international career on a high note. He was in the side which beat Zaire 2-0, and that was his 55th and final cap. He had scored a record 30 goals for his country, a record that has never been beaten.

In August 1974, Denis announced his retirement. There was much speculation that he would go into management but, as he had always said, he was not at all interested in doing that — and he kept his word. Today he still lives in the Manchester area, has several business interests and is in constant demand for personal appearances, after-dinner speaking and for media work.

On a personal note, I have always found Denis to be a wonderful person to have on your side — and an absolute nightmare to be playing against. It is no wonder that he was, and still is, so popular. As a lad he was quite amazing. To be a British record signing when you are just turned 20 is a pretty good assessment of your talent — and what a talent the Lawman had!

I think that his transfer to Italy was probably ill-timed because he was too young to be on his own in such an environment. John Charles had gone to Italy and had been very successful — but he was an older and far more experienced player. At the time that Denis was transferred he was still really a boy genius. If it had all happened two or three years later he would have made at least as great an impact as had John Charles. As it happened, however, Denis was quickly disenchanted and could hardly wait to get back to Britain. I think he would have rowed back himself if only someone had loaned him a boat.

Although he was a star before he left, I personally think that his career really took off when he returned as a Manchester United player. He had it all — brilliant skill, courage and lightning speed. His flowing blond hair was a bonus that made him even more striking and who could ever forget that straight one-arm salute whenever he scored a goal.

I had the pleasure of being able to play alongside him in the Scotland team and, whenever he was in your team, you always felt that you were in with the chance of hitting some goals. He could score spectacular volleys, diving headers or simple tap-ins. If the ball was in the box then the Lawman was in pursuit.

With 30 goals in 55 full internationals, Denis Law is — taking an average — the greatest scorer Scotland's national side has ever known. He used to be really pumped up before a game — every game. He particularly hated England and always wanted to beat them in style. In fact he saw England as the enemy so fiercely that, on the afternoon of the 1966 World Cup Final, he went off to play a game of golf. It wasn't because he was so passionate about golf, but that he couldn't raise the slightest bit of interest in watching England play in the World Cup Final.

Off the park you will never hear anyone have a bad word for Denis Law. He is a very jovial character, always ready for a laugh and a really bubbly person. In short, he is a great guy! But play against him at your peril. All he ever saw were two sides — his own and the enemy. You could be his best pal off the pitch, but if you were wearing an opposition shirt he would be just as likely to kick ten bells out of you. It was not that he was a dirty player — far from it — but he was rugged, hard if you like. He was certainly determined and had no more interest in coming second than a commando on a raid. The story of Jekyll and Hyde could have been based on Denis. He didn't have to drink any strange potion — he just had to pull on a pair of football boots and he was instantly trans-formed from Mr Nice Guy to the Demon King, a nickname he earned during his days with Manchester United.

Denis Law was the man with the hair of gold, quicksilver feet and a diamond heart — one of the very greatest soccer heroes ever to be born in Scotland.

I often bump into Denis and enjoy having a chat about the game that was and the game that is. Like the rest of us he has a few more lines on his face but you can still pick him out of a crowd now just as you could when he was among a crowd of defenders in days gone by.

The Lawman never changes!

Slim Jim

SOCCER heroes do not come any greater than Jim Baxter. The man was, and still is, a legend among legends — an icon to Scottish soccer fans whichever team they happen to support. Like so many of the Scottish greats, he emerged from humble beginnings and rose to the sort of status that is usually reserved for people like Robert the Bruce, Bonnie Prince Charlie or Robbie Burns.

James Curran Baxter was born on 29 September 1939 in a little mining village in Fife. It went by the quaint name of Hill O'Beath — but the name was the only quaint thing about it. Jim was an only child, the son of a miner, and he too seemed destined for life in the darkness of the pit. At least, it seemed that way until someone discovered that he held a passport to a better life — he could really play football.

"At school that's all we wanted to do — play football," recalled Jim. "If there was just five minutes going begging we would fill it with a game of football."

Oddly enough, even though he was so obviously talented — even at that age — it was not until he was almost due to leave school — Cowdenbeath High — that he actually made the school's first team.

"I was too skinny, I suppose," said Jim. He was probably right because there was always an endless stream of soccer scouts watching those school games, and yet not one senior club would take a chance on him. In the end he began his working life down in the mines with his father — but he was not going to be doing that for very long.

There was one scout who had seen him playing for Halbeath Boys' Club who felt that here was a talent which should not be allowed to go to waste. That scout was Willie Butchart of Fife junior side, Crossgates Primrose. He urged Crossgates to sign Baxter and they took his advice. He cost them the legitimate fee of £2 10s (£2.50) — but they also slipped him an extra £30, which he passed on to his mother so that she could buy a washing machine. That was the beginning of one of the strangest careers in soccer.

Don't be fooled by the name — Crossgates Primrose was a tough side and helped in Jim Baxter's early, formative years. Soon he was on his way to the Scottish League and, at the age of 18, he was invited to join Raith Rovers as a part-time professional. Baxter found it necessary to continue as a miner in order to supplement his income. Today he would be hardpushed to keep up with his income — but in the late 1950s, footballer's salaries were still severely restricted.

Bert Herdman was manager of Raith when Baxter joined in 1957 in a £200 deal. Herdman knew that he had found a gem.

"His fantastic confidence attracted me almost as much as his ability," said the then Raith boss.

He had a point. Jim Baxter was one of those footballers who either won an army of fans for his skill — or a legion of enemies for his sheer arrogance. He was said to be big-headed, cocky, flash ...you name it and you can guarantee that he's been called it. The actual truth is that he was simply being what he was — Jim Baxter, a supremely confident, professional footballer — who had the dazzling ability to match his arrogance.

I believe that all truly great players must have that streak of arrogance. It is almost a trademark — a kind of artistic temperament. I'll give you an example of Baxter's approach to the game. When we were both in the Scotland side, playing against Italy, he was not just interested in winning. As we sat in the dressing-room before the game, he turned to me and said: "If I don't put five or six nutmegs on Rivera today, then I won't have had a decent game!"

Now at that time, Rivera was one of the world's greatest players and nobody — but nobody — would think of putting a ball through his legs even once in a lifetime — let alone five or six times in a game. But that was Baxter's whole approach to life — and did he do it? ...He certainly did!

The game wasn't very old before Jim nutmegged Rivera. "That's one!" He shouted to me, and a few minutes later he repeated the performance — "That's two!" Rivera was completely confused. He just didn't know what was going on. I knew — but I still couldn't believe what I was seeing happen before my eyes.

Jim Baxter made progress at Raith. The Stark's Park supporters knew that they had something special in their midst and it came as no surprise when he was called up for the Scotland under-23 side. His debut for Scotland was not one of his better performances but he persevered and his club form certainly continued to become even more of a revelation. When the mighty Rangers were the visitors in 1958, Baxter played well above even his own high standard and Raith chalked up a 3-1 victory. Many followers of football say that that match was Jim's finest hour in the Scottish League.

Rangers fans would probably argue that point — not just because it was they who were on the receiving end — but also because Baxter became a Rangers player himself in the summer of 1960. Thus began the greatest era of his career. Raith received a payment of £17,500 for Baxter, which was a huge fee then.

The arrival of Baxter provided Rangers with a new lease of life. Make no mistake, the Ibrox club was on a roll but Baxter was a major new piece in the jig-saw. The fans loved his skill and were absolutely smitten by his style. In those days he was quite slightly built and it did not take long for the 'Slim Jim' nick-name to stick. With Baxter at left-half, Rangers went from strength to strength and, over the next few years, they won just about everything that was going — including three League championships, two Scottish Cup victories and four Scottish League Cup triumphs.

Jim Baxter was the focal point for the fan's adulation in Glasgow and he also very quickly became a national hero with his displays for Scotland. In 1963 he made his first-ever Wembley appearance and he scored the two goals that gave Scotland such a memorable victory. Even though one of those goals was a penalty, the Baxter legend reached new heights. In 1964 he played at Wembley again, this time for the Rest of the World against England. Once again his play was majestic as he rubbed shoulders with the very best in world football.

Baxter was much more than a brilliantly talented footballer — he was also a great entertainer and liked to play to the gallery. He loved beating Celtic — and, of course, England. After one cup final match between the two 'Old Firm' sides, he led the victory celebrations by grabbing the match-ball and stuffing it up his shirt. The fans loved it and he loved it too.

"If you're good at something and you're paid to do it, then why not give value for money?" he said.

The party was ruined in December 1964 when Rangers were playing away to Rapid Vienna in the European Cup, second-round tie. Baxter had won the 70,000 Austrian fans over with his skill but, in the last minute of the game, an ill-timed tackle broke his leg. Rangers had won with a 3-1 aggregate score-line, but the loss of the brilliant Baxter was a heavy price to pay.

As a result of his accident Baxter was, of course, out of action for some months — during which time Rangers were eliminated from the European Cup by Inter-Milan. They also failed to win the Scottish championship for a third successive time, ending the season in fifth position. Only the Scottish League Cup was retained and in May 1965, after he had finally recovered from the accident, Baxter agreed to make a fresh start with a new club.

Rangers pocketed £75,000 from the deal — the highest fee ever received by a Scottish club up to then. Baxter admitted that the move was chiefly motivated by a need for money, as he explained at the time.

"Go into Wylie and Lochhead in Glasgow and order a three-piece suite, a bedroom suite and a fitted carpet," he said. "Then tell the salesman, when he asks about payment, that you've got so many Scottish Cup medals, lots of inter-national caps and some championship medals, and he'll look at you as if you're round the bend!"

Players' salaries were not then what they are today and there are few who could argue with Baxter's candid explan-ation of the situation. He was 26 years of age and had just recovered from a broken leg which, although he still felt invincible on the field of play, made him realise his vulner-ability and that he wouldn't be playing football for ever. Foot-ballers today earn more in a week than would have taken players of that era five or six seasons to gain. Looking at things in that light, no-one could blame Baxter for following a quest for personal financial security.

In all honesty Jim was never quite the same after his broken leg — judged by his own incredible standards. How-ever he was still a star. If anything was lacking it was in the consistency of form that had been so spell-binding in Scotland.

Sunderland was the new club and, like anyone who was transferred from a Scottish club, Baxter found the English Football League to be a bit of a culture shock. It was much more demanding physically and of a higher standard gen-erally. There were certainly times when the Sunderland fans had to rub their eyes as Baxter's magic unfolded before them — but he no longer turned it on quite as often as he had in Scotland.

While at Roker Park he added a further ten caps to his Scotland career, including the famous 1967 international against England — about which we shall have more to say later on. He played 88 League games for Sunderland and scored ten goals. During his time there he charmed the fans but the Rokermen were no better off for cups and medals. However, his performance there was enough to interest Nottingham Forest and make them want a slice of his action. They were prepared to make the astonishing offer of £100,000 for the 28-year-old player, whose displays of magic were now only coming in touches rather than in prolonged spells.

It was in December 1967 when Baxter pulled on a Forest shirt for the first time. Johnny Carey was his new manager and the City Ground fans were thrilled at seeing the Scottish sensation in their colours ...It didn't last though!

Off the park, as well as on it, Jim Baxter was a law unto himself. Make no mistake, he was never an abusive person — except, perhaps, to himself. You'd never find him wasting his time getting into trouble. He simply loved life and enjoyed his drink. He was an extremely exuberant character who loved to socialise.

He was a genius at his work and, like all geniuses, he lived life to the full during his time off. He worked extremely hard during training in an attempt to compensate for all his excesses off the pitch but the 'Slim Jim' of yesteryear had given way to a much weightier version. He stayed less than two years at the City Ground — eventually being given a free transfer after there had been no takers at £40,000, and then later at £20,000. He had played only 48 League games for Forest and when new manager, Matt Gillies, finally released him, the statisticians worked out that he had cost the club about £2,000 a game — chicken-feed now, but an expensive commodity then.

That was by no means the end of the Baxter story. His

return to Scotland was comparable with troops returning home after a war. Rangers took him home on the free transfer deal and, amid a blaze of publicity, he was reunited with the staunchest of his fans. He went on to play a further 15 games for Rangers in that 1969-70 season — and even managed a couple of goals — but it was to be his swan-song.

At the end of the season he was made available again on a free transfer. The Light Blues had had a change of management with Willie Waddell taking the hot seat and Jock Wallace being appointed coach. Baxter did not figure in their plans. He was not particularly upset but, by the same token, he did not want to slide down the scale until he found himself struggling to make it in a lower division. He was 30 years of age, had experienced a lifetime in soccer and now felt ready to start a new life without his football boots.

Jim, his wife Jean, and their two sons remained in Glasgow where he bought a pub. Naturally, that pub became a mecca for soccer fans — and not only for Scottish soccer fans either. Football followers from all over Britain, and even further afield, flocked there to meet the great man, get an autograph, and to talk.

Jim became accustomed to their questions and never shirked giving honest replies. Here was a man who had got the world at his feet — so why on earth did he allow his high-performance social life drive his soccer career off the road?

"What did I do? — I enjoyed myself, that's what!" Jim admitted. "Don't talk to me about regrets …I haven't got any. Anyone who goes around moaning about what they should, or shouldn't, have done in the past needs to see a head-shrinker. D'you know something? If I had my time all over again, I'd probably be exactly the same." Even in his retirement, Jim Baxter never lost what some described as arrogance. He had an explanation for that too:- "I know I've been called arrogant — well, maybe that's how it looked to some and I can't help what people say. But I'll tell you a story about that. When I was about 18, I was picked for the Scotland under-23 side — my first cap. It was against Wales at Tynecastle and it was a big day for me.

"I was with Raith then. I go over to Edinburgh, full of myself of course, and all togged out in my best gear. When I see the other lads from Glasgow and England, they really look something and suddenly I feel like a country yokel — a nobody. All the kids are queuing up for their autographs. I'm asked a couple of times for mine — but when I sign I see them looking at it to see who I am. Well, that was the day I made up my mind that I was going to be noticed. I knew that I could play but I had to make sure that everybody else knew as well. But I can promise you this, I never attempted anything on the field that I wasn't confident of being able to bring off."

I can vouch for that. Jim was a fantastic player. He never really boasted because he could, and would, do all that he said he could. He was a terrific guy to have on your side and an absolute nightmare to play against. He could simply shrug his shoulders and the opposition would be wrong-footed. He was a master of his craft.

In recent years Jim has given up the pub, mostly due to ill-health. He had an operation not too long ago, probably as a result of his earlier life-style. Was he a fool? Some people might well say so. I would say that it was all his own business. He knew what he was doing and he chose his own path.

He always loved life and led it to the full, lighting up everyone else's life while he was in their company.

Today, Jim is taking things a little easier. He is still an icon to Scottish soccer fans. To me he will always be a pure genius of football.

Sweet and Sour Souness

IF EVER there was a soccer wolf in sheep's clothing it would be Graeme Souness. When he became manager of Southampton in the summer of 1996 and returned to Anfield with his new side, he received a very mixed welcome. For some fans he was the culprit of a bad patch for Liverpool, whom he managed from 1991 to 1994. For others he was worthy of a standing ovation. The latter remembered his other Anfield years — as a Liverpool player ...and what a player!

Graeme Souness was never a stargazer. There was never any front about him. He simply went out believing that he could beat anyone — and usually he did!

The Souness story began in Edinburgh where he was born on 6 May 1953. You would probably never imagine someone like Graeme Souness getting homesick yet, like so many other young Scots, he did and it even caused questions to be asked in the House of Commons.

Souness left school in Edinburgh as a 15-year-old and was lured by the bright city lights of London and the high-profile tradition of Tottenham Hotspur. Everyone at White Hart Lane was very enthusiastic and looked upon him as the new Dave Mackay, of whom we shall have more to say later. For Souness the teenager, the excitement of being in London with one of the world's most famous clubs did not last very long.

At the age of 17, he wilted under the strain of missing his family, his friends and his home back in Edinburgh, and walked out on Tottenham. He returned to Scotland. His club reacted by slapping a two-week suspension without pay on him. His local MP thought that it was an outrage for a young lad, under the stress of homesickness, to be treated so harshly by the club and actually raised the point in Parliament.

Once home, however, Souness began to consider what he had done and also how much he really did want a career in soccer. He relented, healed the rift with Tottenham manager Bill Nicholson, and returned to White Hart Lane with renewed determination to do his best in his chosen profession.

Although he continued to make progress at Tottenham, his talents were never given the chance to blossom at first-team level and in December 1972, Middlesbrough — then living in the shadow of rivals Newcastle and Sunderland — bought him for £27,000. That seems a paltry sum now, but it was not a bad fee all those years ago and it was a real testimony to Middlesbrough that they had such faith in the potential of a player who had not yet played a first-team game.

To say that he had not made the Tottenham first team at all is not strictly true. He did make one appearance as a substitute in a European tie. Nevertheless, Middlesbrough had had very little chance to see how he would be able to cope with the rigours of senior football. Before very long 'Boro threw Graeme in at the deep end. He made his debut on the day that he signed — 30 December 1972. It was a home match which ended with Middlesbrough beating Oxford United 1-0 — so Souness went back to his digs with a big smile on his face.

A few months after Graeme arrived at Middlesbrough, in May 1973 to be exact, the club appointed a new manager, my old Leeds team-mate Jack Charlton. While all credit for gambling on Souness in the first place goes to Stan Anderson, it must be said that his career really took off under the guidance of Big Jack.

"It was obvious that Graeme had enormous potential but that he was being played out of position," said Jack. "He was played as a left-sided midfielder or a full-back, which occasionally emphasised his lack of pace. I moved him into the central midfield position and tried to make him a more positive player.

"His main fault was that he always tended to dwell on the ball for too long — consequently being forced to pass the ball backwards instead of forward. He seemed to have the idea that good players should try to look clever on the ball and for two years I constantly nagged at him to cut down on this tendency to over-elaborate."

Jack's coaching certainly worked. By May 1974 Middlesbrough were champions of the old Second Division and the Scotland selectors were taking a very close look at Graeme, who was playing such a major part in his club's success. Big Jack had no doubts about where Graeme's career could lead.

He said at the time, "If Graeme plays to his full ability he can win many honours. That ability is a gift to any team. The only thing he needs to curb is an arrogant streak that can sometimes surface in his play."

Jack was right of course, Graeme Souness went all the way to the top.

As success at Middlesbrough ebbed and flowed, there was the usual speculation about players coming and going but there was only one direction for Graeme Souness. He was a rising star. He got his Scotland chance on 30 October 1974 against East Germany in Glasgow. I was not playing in that one but I was there to see the Scotland team record a great 3-0 victory. The East Germans were no push-overs — it was a great result. Among the scorers was a guy by the name of Dalglish and, from that moment on, it seemed that the names of Souness and Dalglish were often going to appear together.

I was in the side for Graeme's next match. He had worn the No.4 shirt for the match with East Germany but when we played Spain on 20 November 1974, his was the No.7 shirt while I pulled on my familiar No.6. We lost 2-1, but it was a good game and could quite easily have gone either way. We were by no means discredited by the result. I can remember being in the dressing-room before kick-off as we were all changing, getting instructions and generally geeing each other up. One of the quietest was Graeme Souness. He kept himself to himself, smiled when there was a joke but never got too involved.

It was not that Graeme was anti-social. It was simply that he became totally focused on the job in hand. His mind was fully concentrated and he did not welcome any distractions.

He did not appear to get nervous — in fact there was almost an air of invincibility around him to match the confidence of Jim Baxter.

That was the only time that I can remember actually lining up at the start of a Scotland game with Graeme, although we were squad mates on a number of occasions. In training he was dedicated, hard-working and, I can only use that same description again, totally focused. I thought at the time that he was going to become one of Scotland's greats and I don't think that anyone could seriously deny that he did.

In all, Graeme won 54 caps — the same as me. Like me he became captain of Scotland and was probably the best-ever. After his first few games for his country he fell out of the reckoning for a while but finally returned in February 1978 for a 2-1 win over Bulgaria and thereafter became a Scotland regular. He took part in three World Cup finals — 1978, 1982 and 1986 — and was outstanding in each tournament.

Probably his finest hour for Scotland was at Hampden in 1984. I was there that night as well. It was ten years after his first cap and he had realised all that potential. He was captain of the side and led them magnificently as they destroyed Yugoslavia 6-1. He never missed a tackle, never failed to keep his troops on their toes — and even got on the score-sheet. It was a game to remember for Souness and for everyone who saw his magnificent performance at Hampden that day.

I was not the only one to be impressed by Graeme. Bob Paisley at Liverpool had seen him a number of times and decided that he was well worth an investment — which is why, on 11 January 1978, Souness signed on the dotted line and became a Liverpool player. He also became a record-breaker, as the £352,000 was a record deal between two English clubs at that time.

A few days after the big news transfer, Souness donned a Liverpool shirt for the first time and delighted the Reds fans with his part in a 1-0 win over West Bromwich Albion. For those who like statistics, it was on 14 January 1978 — and among those in the Liverpool line-up was one Kenny Dalglish. Now they really were team-mates and Liverpool was entering one of the most successful periods in the club's history. I like to think that the presence of Souness, Dalglish, and another Scot — Alan Hansen, was one of the prime reasons for so much silverware finding its way to Anfield.

Things can happen very quickly in football. Only four months after pulling on a Liverpool shirt for the first time, Graeme found himself walking out at Wembley to face FC Bruges in the European Cup Final. To say that it was a big occasion would be an understatement — but he thrived on big occasions and was certainly not phased by this one.

"I had already made my European debut — twice," Graeme explained. "People talked about my European debut when I went on as a substitute against Borussia Moenchen-gladnbach in the first leg of the European Cup semi-final, on 29 March 1978. They had forgotten that my real debut was when I was 18, when I went on as a substitute for Martin Peters about 30 minutes from the end of Tottenham's UEFA Cup tie in Iceland during the 1971-72 season.

"I never dreamed then that I would one day be playing for the full game in the European Cup Final — or that I would put the pass through that paved the way for the winning goal!"

But that is exactly what happened as millions tuned into

their televisions and radios to see if Liverpool could really pull it off. But before we start assuming that Graeme's Anfield career was one glittering success after another, let us consider his first few weeks there — because it is to his credit that he came through a difficult time.

Of course, Liverpool did win the European Cup with that single goal to become the first British side ever to retain the trophy. It was by no means the last such success that Souness was going to experience. As his Anfield career progressed he became skipper of the side and, by the time that he was transferred to Sampdoria — in June 1984 for £650,000 — he had enjoyed six years of solid gold soccer glory.

When he packed his bags for Italy he was the richer by three European Cup winners medals, five League championship medals and four League Cup medals. He was given a rousing send-off but it was not to be the last time that he would be on the Liverpool staff, although the second time it was as manager.

Souness the player had earned the reputation of being very tough in the tackle, quick-thinking when he was in possession and more than capable when there was the chance to put the ball in the back of the net. He was respected throughout the game, adored by the Liverpool fans and revered by Scots all over the country. He was fiery on the pitch and quiet off it and there was no denying that he was highly motivated by a sheer passion for the game. He was a winner.

After two enjoyable years with Sampdoria, Souness returned to Britain in a surprise move which saw him become player-manager of Rangers. It is fair to say that the fantastic run enjoyed by the Ibrox club in the last decade owes much to the revolutionary management style of Graeme Souness. He gave Rangers back their pride and injected new ideas into the club. It wasn't just ideas either.

Graeme's presence attracted an invasion of English stars like Mark Hateley, Chris Woods, Terry Butcher, Trevor Francis, Ray Wilkins, Mark Walters and Nigel Spackman. The Rangers revolution worked as the trophies began to roll in, along with the crowds. It was not all plain sailing of course — you can't expect cucumber sandwiches in the dressing-room when you have someone with the gutsy fire of Graeme Souness calling the shots.

On his playing debut for Rangers he was sent off — but it was almost a badge of honour compared with the pre-Souness era which had seen more of a low-profile, jolly hockey-sticks approach to the game. That opening game showed that Souness was still the same swashbuckling soccer star that he had always been.

When Kenny Dalglish announced his shock resignation from the manager's chair at Anfield, press and public alike instantly called for Souness to be appointed. Rangers fans were horrified at the prospect of losing their leader — but for Graeme, the challenge was too great to be resisted. He received a hero's welcome when he returned to Anfield — but there were to be stormy times ahead.

What happened at Anfield during those years in which Souness was the boss still remains a mystery. Did he inherit a problem that was greater than had been made public? Did he change his hitherto successful style because of boardroom pressure, or out of sheer ego? Only Graeme knows the answers to these questions. Whatever the reason, the phenomenal success of his years at Ibrox were not to be repeated at Anfield and finally, in January 1994, he parted company with Liverpool under something of a cloud.

In 1995 he became manager of Galatasary and had a successful season there. Surprisingly, his one-year contract was not renewed and he returned to these shores to become manager of Southampton.

Graeme's management career may have had its ups and downs but we are only really concerned with his status as a Scottish soccer hero — based on his playing career. He had a fantastic career as has already been stated. I liked him. I admired his inner strength of mind and his will to win.

Graeme Souness the player was, without a doubt, one of the very best to come out of Scotland. People talk in awe of players like Ian St John and Kenny Dalglish, but for me no list of Scottish soccer heroes would be complete without the name of Graeme Souness being highly placed. He has to be one of the greatest British midfielders of all time.

I played alongside Graeme Souness and I played against him. We met socially a number of times and I have watched his expertise on the pitch on countless occasions. The number of Scotland caps that he has won has earned him a place in the Scottish Football Association's Hall of fame.

In my opinion, if anyone really deserves a hero's place in the history books of Scottish soccer, it is the wholly unique Graeme Souness.

Last Minute Reilly

I AM disappointed to say that I have not played alongside all my Scottish soccer heroes — and I particularly grieve at not having lined up in the same side as Lawrie Reilly, who became known throughout the game as 'Last-minute Reilly'. That label does not stem from situations such as turning up late for training, but from the gritty determination that inspired him to give his all, right up to the very last whistle blast — an attitude that often led him to swing the entire result in the dying minutes of a game.

Lawrie was an Edinburgh lad, born there in October 1928. His childhood years included the usual dosage of street soccer, although there were interruptions between his 11th and 16th birthday as World War Two was in full swing. He blossomed as a prospect with Edinburgh Thistle — a much-respected juvenile club — and, at the age of 16, he was taken on by Hibernian whom he had supported since early childhood.

His career with Hibs spanned 13 years, and there is no doubt that he would have gone on a lot longer if it had not been for the cartilage trouble which forced him into early retirement in 1958 at the age of 29.

Why was he so special?

In short, he was one of the most prolific goal-scorers in the game. For all that goal-scoring ability he was not, at 5ft 7ins, at all typical of the burly, bustling centre-forward that is usually the spearhead of any meaningful attack.

His League record of 185 goals in 253 games gives you some idea of his ability — and yet there was much more to Lawrie Reilly than can be shown by any mere list of statistics. He had strength, speed and determination, together with a keen eye for the half-chance that made him a constant threat to any defence unfortunate enough to have been given the unenviable task of trying to contain him.

Perhaps a few more statistics might help after all. He was the most-capped player that Hibernian have ever had, collecting 38 during his shortened career. He must surely have topped the half-century had he played for a few more years. Those 38 caps yielded 22 goals, which is a record that places him third among Scotland's all-time international goal-scorers, behind Kenny Dalglish and Denis Law who each scored 30. Without seeming to detract from either of these last two, it is worth considering that Denis scored his 30 in 55 appearances, and Kenny collected his in 102. Perhaps that puts Lawrie's total in a better perspective!

Three times he topped the Scottish First Division scorers' table and, in the 1952-53 season, he bagged 50 goals in League, Cup and international matches.

Perhaps that gives the impression that Lawrie Reilly was simply a greedy goal-grabber. He was nothing of the kind …far from it in fact! He was a diligent team member who would always slip the ball to a team-mate if he thought that he had a better chance of planting it in the net.

There was the classic example of his unselfish play at Wembley in 1949 when he was playing for Scotland against England. Scotland won the game 3-1, but it was Lawrie Reilly who set the ball rolling as it were. England opened with a flurry and Jimmy Cowan had to be on top form in the Scotland goal. Gradually, the men in blue began to make their presence felt and, in the 20th minute, Billy Steel sent a great pass to Lawrie Reilly. He carved a hole in the England defence and bore down on goalkeeper Frank Swift. Probably, Reilly could have gone for glory and would almost certainly have scored. Instead, he slipped the ball to Jimmy Mason who was in a position where he could not have possibly missed. It was not only a brilliant move from Reilly, but it typified his attitude of team before personal glory. That goal broke England's heart, Billy Steel grabbed a goal for himself and Lawrie Reilly put the icing on the cake to make it 3-1.

Going back to his club days with Hibs, Lawrie made the first team in the 1946-47 season when he made only five appearances but still scored twice, heralding the future goals still to come. He was only 17 when he made his senior debut and Hibs did not make the mistake of pushing him too far too quickly. The following season he doubled his goal tally, scoring four in only six League appearances. His career really took off in the 1948-49 season, when his 14 goals in 20 League matches forced the hand of the Scotland selectors. The season was not very old when he was picked for his first full international. It was against Wales, in Cardiff, on 23 October 1948. There were celebrations all round. Not only was it his first cap and close to his 20th birthday, but Scotland won the game 3-1.

As he progressed, so Hibernian, also, enjoyed a great spell. They were runners-up to champions Rangers in 1946-47, and then won the title themselves the following season. Having played only six League matches, Reilly was not eligible for a medal but his day was still to come. The 1948-49 season saw Hibernian finish third, and the following season they were runners-up again, one point behind Rangers.

However, Lawrie was not to be denied his medals and, in the 1950-51 and 1951-52 seasons, Hibernian dominated the Scottish First Division, taking the League championship almost with ease on both occasions. In the first of these two seasons they won the Scottish League Cup as well.

One honour that did elude him was the Scottish FA Cup. Hibernian were twice involved in the final during his days at the club, but the first time was in 1947 when he was too young to be included in the side which lost 2-1 to Aberdeen. The second time was at the end of his career in 1958 when his knee injury ruled him out of the game for the rest of his life. He was a spectator as Hibernian lost 1-0 to Clyde.

During his career, Reilly remained a one-club man. For some of that time he was a part-timer, away from football he was a painter by trade. He could probably have earned much more if he had tried his luck in England, but Lawrie was not really interested in stardom. He enjoyed his football but never really looked upon it as a serious career.

That thought did not reflect in his style of play, however. He never stopped working during a game and he never stopped thinking either. He was lightning-fast, both in actions and in thoughts. His former team-mate, Willie Ormond, once described him as a unique centre-forward.

"They simply don't make them like that anymore," said Willie. "Lawrie Reilly was of a different breed because he was always willing to add something extra in order to get a goal. He was prepared to be hurt, just so long as he could get the ball into the net. Maybe you wouldn't call him especially elegant — but what an exciting player! He was a great man to have on your side. He had guts — and I would say that he was the ultimate professional."

There is something that Willie did not mention — and that is how Lawrie became known as 'Last-minute Reilly'. It was a nick-name given to him by the Easter Road fans who thrilled to his exploits on the pitch. He never stopped trying and earned dozens of goals simply by keeping going — right to the very last whistle blast. His reputation reached new heights in 1953 when his never-say-die approach saw him score a very late equaliser for Scotland against England at Wembley. He was prepared to keep going while others wilted, and he reaped the benefit when his late shot eluded Gil Merrick in the England goal and forced a 2-2 draw. Just for the record, Lawrie had scored Scotland's earlier goal too!

Hibernian were the first British club to enter the European Cup when it began in the 1955-56 season. They reached the semi-finals before going out to Reims and, of course, Lawrie Reilly's name was among the goal-scorers in that pioneering campaign.

It was a great loss when Lawrie had to call it a day. He never lost contact with, or interest in, Hibernian however and was even offered a directorship when he retired. He declined that honour, but he continued to take advantage of the seat that was always reserved for him at Easter Road in the directors' box. Basically, he went back to being a supporter.

For income, he ran a pleasant little pub in Leith and it was a rare evening that there was nobody to seek his opinions or delve into his memories.

On a personal note, I remember going to see Lawrie play for both Hibernian and Scotland. What an exciting player. He was not called 'Last-minute Reilly' for nothing. His energy and zest were fantastic. He had a real 'Roy of the Rovers' image, especially with that so-appropriate nick-name. He really did score a lot of late match-winners and final throw-of-the-dice equalisers.

Hibernian had a brilliant forward line in those days — possibly the best ever seen in Scotland. Gordon Smith, Bobby Johnstone, Eddie Turnbull, Willie Ormond and, of course, Lawrie Reilly were football's 'Famous Five' north of the border. It was a marvellous attack and was all home-grown — unlike the talented line-ups of today which seem more like the 'Rest of the World XI'.

When you stop to consider the facilities and the equipment of that age, it makes you wonder just how good those stars of yesteryear might have been today. The boots were tougher leather and the ball was equally as uncompromising. After a while on a muddy pitch, it took great leg muscles to heave a ball into the goal area from the corner flag

— and even greater skull-structure and neck muscles to head that ball as it plummeted down to earth.

Ball control in those days was possibly even more difficult than it is today — and it would be fascinating to see how those stars would play with the lighter ball and footwear of today.

Lawrie Reilly would doubtless have made just as great an impression. His fantastic touch on the ball would be just as devastating if he was bare-footed and the ball was square. In addition to his skill he was an outstanding worker, and that alone would have made him a top star today.

Having been a fan before he became a player, and then a fan again after he had hung up his boots, you might expect that he would still be following the fortunes of Hibernian. Naturally, you would be right! He is still as keen as ever and often takes his special seat at Easter Road. Youngsters who might not recognise him on sight are soon educated by their elders.

"That's Lawrie Reilly — 'Last-minute Reilly' — he was one of the greatest players that Scotland has ever produced!"

He is also an all-time hero of yours truly!

Jackie Mudie
–Unsung Hero

MATTHEWS and Mortensen are still mentioned in hushed tones throughout English football as they are revered by generation after generation. That is natural enough — they were both great players and fully deserving of the applause that has echoed down through the ages. But there was another of Blackpool's 'M-people' who has, in my opinion, been forced to live in the shadow of these two football stars down through the years. I think that it is now time for the spotlight to focus on him — and so, Jackie Mudie is numbered among my Scottish soccer heroes as a tribute to a player who was nothing short of brilliant.

The Jackie Mudie story began in Dundee where he was born on 10 April 1930. One of seven brothers, he was a little lad like myself, he loved football and ran rings around boys who were much bigger and older than himself. By the time that he was getting into senior school he was already playing with adults, as an amateur with Lochee Harp, and then with Stobswell Juniors.

It was just after World War Two that he came to the attention of Blackpool and, in June 1947, he signed professional forms with them. His first name was really John but, like so many of that era, John became converted to Jack and Jack eventually became Jackie.

He took the move to Blackpool in his stride and did not appear to suffer from those same bouts of homesickness that so many others of us Scots did when we moved south of the border. Perhaps it was being in Blackpool that helped. The town has long been a popular seaside resort among Scots. There were probably very few days that Jackie would not hear a familiar accent from his home country as he walked along the prom.

Naturally, as a young lad he still had a lot to learn, and it was nearly three years before he finally made the Blackpool first team. However, it was a debut that was worth waiting for since it was away to Liverpool in March 1950. He ran the Liverpool defence ragged — and stunned Anfield fans when he scored the only goal of the game. It was a dream debut for the young inside-forward, and it set him on the road to stardom.

The Blackpool fans quickly took to him and, in his first full season, he not only played his part in his team's third place finish in the 1950-51 First Division table — behind champions Tottenham and runners-up Manchester United — but he also helped them all the way to Wembley and the FA Cup Final against Newcastle.

The excitement of a day out at Wembley fizzled to a disappointing end when the Blackpool players collected their losers' medals — two goals from Jackie Milburn winning the game for Newcastle. However, Blackpool, together with Jackie Mudie, were destined to come back.

For a while Mudie played second fiddle to Stan Morten-sen, but his displays in training and for the reserves were such that manager Joe Smith finally had to accommodate both men in the first team. The reward came in 1953 when Jackie scored a last-minute winner against Tottenham in the FA Cup semi-final and assured his side of another trip to Wembley. It was Coronation year, Everest was conquered and Hungary demonstrated to England the way to play football. Before all of that, however, in May of that year, it was the Matthews Final!

Bolton were winning 3-1 after 68 minutes, but then Stan Matthews turned it on and combined with Stan Mortensen to get Blackpool back in the game — and ultimately win it with a score of 4-3. Those brilliant Matthews skills were the talk of soccer but Stan himself was always extremely quick to remind everyone that it was a team effort, and that Jackie Mudie was an outstanding member of that team.

"Jackie Mudie was a great player," said Stan. "He was a real live-wire and never stopped working for the team. He was a tremendous scorer but totally unselfish — often doing all the hard work and then passing the chance for glory on to someone else."

That's how I remember Mudie as well. His ability to score goals really came to the fore after the transfer of Stan Mort-ensen to Hull in 1955. Mudie took over the No.9 shirt and, in his first season as the club's official centre-forward, he scored 20 goals. In his second season he really went to town and scored 32 — which is still a post-war club record, I believe!

Jackie Mudie remained a Blackpool player until Stoke paid £8,500 for him in 1960. He scored after just five minutes in his debut for them. During his Blackpool days, Jackie played in 320 League matches and scored 143 goals. He had lost nothing of his magic touch when he played for Stoke, although he was by that time 30 years of age. During two and a half years at the Victoria Ground he hit 32 goals in 89 games, and helped them to promotion into the First Division, linking up again, of course, with the great Stan Matthews who had returned to the Potters with whom he had begun his career before the war.

Mudie left Stoke in November 1963 and went the few miles to Port Vale, where he remained until 1966 — chalking up nine goals in 54 games. He had two seasons there as player-manager.

My own memories of Jackie Mudie are not from League football but from his prowess as a Scottish international. I suppose that there are few people who would think of including him in their list of heroes, but he was a huge favourite of mine so I hope you will excuse my self-indulgence. I used to love watching him play for Scotland. All his caps were won while he was a Blackpool player and he certainly took part in some memorable matches.

His first cap was in October 1956, in a Home International against Wales in Cardiff. Lawrie Reilly was playing alongside him and it was Lawrie who scored one of Scotland's goals in the 2-2 draw — Bill Fernie getting the other. Less than a month later Mudie was on international duty once again, making his Hampden debut. I remember the game well. He had a great match and seemed to be everywhere at once. Northern Ireland were the visitors and found him to be a real handful. Scotland won the match 1-0, but it was an excellent performance against a good Northern Ireland side which included such stars as Danny and Jackie Blanchflower, Jimmy McIlroy, Billy Bingham, Peter McParland and Harry Gregg.

In Mudie's next international he scored his first Scotland goal. It was against Yugoslavia at Hampden Park on 21 November 1956. How about that for a memory? I was there! Scotland won 2-0 with Jackie Mudie and Sam Baird scoring the goals. In his total of 17 games for Scotland, Jackie Mudie scored nine goals. He played in the 1958 World Cup finals in Sweden, but probably his finest hour came on the qualifying road to that tournament.

I was there when Spain came to Hampden on 8 May 1957 for a World Cup qualifier. Everyone knew that Spain would provide fierce opposition but somehow they must have forgotten to tell Jackie Mudie. With thousands of Scots roaring him on, Jackie ran the Spaniards ragged. Not only did he carve up the Spanish defence like a hot knife slicing through butter, but he also hit a fantastic hat-trick. Scotland won 4-2, the other Scottish goal coming from a John Hewie penalty — and that result virtually bought the tickets for Sweden.

In the World Cup tournament Scotland failed to get past the group stage. Jackie scored against Paraguay but it was to be his last goal for his country. The following game ended in a 2-1 defeat against France. He had a hand in Sam Baird's goal for Scotland, but it was a farewell performance. A new era of Scottish football was dawning with names like Law and St John about to emerge.

I had the pleasure of meeting Jackie Mudie at a function in Dublin not long before he died in 1992. Stanley Matthews was there too. I went up to him feeling rather like a schoolboy meeting a big star for the first time.

"Of all the people that I ever wanted to meet, you are number 1," I said. "You have been my hero for years!"

Stan Matthews butted in and said: "You see Jackie — you are famous!"

"**** off!" Jackie replied, good naturedly. He wasn't intending to be dismissive or rude — he was simply a very modest man who was more than happy to remain in the background while others claimed the spotlight.

Another thing that struck me was his size. As you know, I am no giant — but Jackie was three or four inches shorter than me. How could a man of his height be so magnificent in the air? Many of his goals came from headers and he had this amazing ability to out-jump much taller defenders and to, seemingly, almost hover in the air.

When Jackie Mudie died on 2 March 1992, it was at his home in Stoke — where he had settled among the people who had adopted him as one of their own. He had been ill with cancer for about two years but, just as he had played his football, he refused to give in until that final whistle blast.

His friend, Stanley Matthews, paid tribute by saying, "Jackie was one of the real heroes of football. His skill and work for others often made some of us look better than we really were."

Jackie was a hero all right — a Scottish soccer hero.

The Duke of York (later King George VI) meets the Scottish team before the game at Wembley in 1928. Less than two hours later this team would be forever known as the Wembley Wizards and a legend was born.

England goalkeeper Ted Hufton is beaten yet again, this time by Hughie Gallacher, as Scotland hammer the English for five goals, a day which still lives in the annals of Scottish football history.

Hughie Gallacher, a genius of a footballer who hailed from Bellshill, an area which proved a rich seam of Scottish soccer talent over the years.

Lawrie Reilly scores for Scotland at Wembley, eluding Billy Wright's tackle as he shoots. The other players nearest the camera (from left to right) are Byrne, Johnstone, Edwards and Ring.

Little Jackie Mudie, seen here in the colours of Stoke City. Jackie was one of the true unsung heroes of the game. The Dundee-born inside-forward was perhaps overshadowed by the likes of Matthews and Mortensen when he was at Blackpool, was nevertheless one of the game's most brilliant performers.

Dave Mackay, in the shirt of Tottenham Hotspur, the club with which his name is synonymous. He helped them win the League and Cup double in England in 1961. Winning meant everything to Dave and he should have played for Scotland many more times than he did.

Rangers and Scotland skipper George Young, a true colossus of the game and one of the players whose presence dominated Scottish football after World War Two.

Alex Young, the 'Golden Vision'. He started with Hearts and later moved to Goodison Park, where his name is still revered by Everton fans. He would have made a great manager or coach.

Willie Henderson, a winger who created enormous excitement wherever he played – and struck fear into the hearts of opposing defenders. He was one of the great Scottish players who showed that there could be a better life beyond the tenements of Glasgow.

Jim Baxter, who had that streak of arrogance that all truly great footballers must possess. The fans adored him and he is still an icon among followers of the game north of the border.

There have been few sights in football to match the little Celtic and Scotland winger Jimmy Johnstone in full flight. Jimmy was a star when Celtic won the European Cup in 1967.

Tommy Gemmell's shot scorches past a leaping Sarti in the Inter-Milan goal during the 1967 European Cup Final in Lisbon.

Celtic skipper Billy McNeill is mobbed by Celtic fans after his team's epic victory. It's hard to think that it is 30 years since that wonderful night for Scottish football.

Billy McNeill leads out Celtic in 1969. They called him Caesar and he was a real giant of a player. He looked even bigger when he was holding aloft a trophy – which was quite often.

The oldest player on the pitch, Ronnie Simpson (36) and the youngest, Jim McCalliog (20) congratulate each other after Scotland's victory over World Champions England at Wembley in 1967.

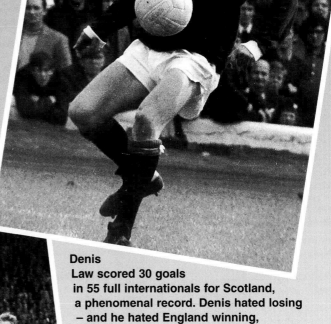

Denis Law scored 30 goals in 55 full internationals for Scotland, a phenomenal record. Denis hated losing – and he hated England winning, whoever they were playing!

Your's truly in action for Scotland with Denis Law looking on. I was fortunate enough to win 54 caps for my country, one less than the Lawman.

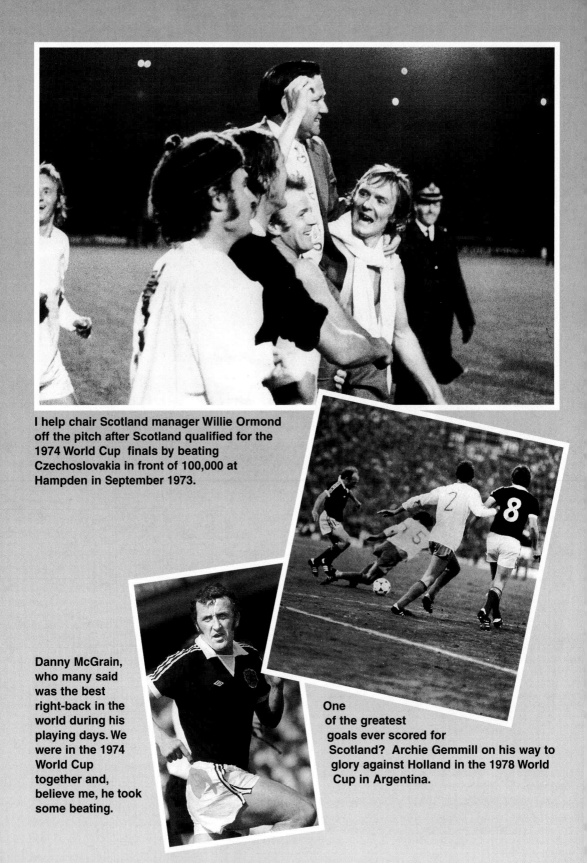

I help chair Scotland manager Willie Ormond off the pitch after Scotland qualified for the 1974 World Cup finals by beating Czechoslovakia in front of 100,000 at Hampden in September 1973.

Danny McGrain, who many said was the best right-back in the world during his playing days. We were in the 1974 World Cup together and, believe me, he took some beating.

One of the greatest goals ever scored for Scotland? Archie Gemmill on his way to glory against Holland in the 1978 World Cup in Argentina.

Kenny Dalglish beats Holland's goalkeeper Jongbloed to score Scotland's first goal against the Dutch in the 1978 World Cup finals. Whatever accolades are heaped on Kenny, he deserves every one of them.

Graeme Souness in the blue of Scotland. Graeme went about the field believing he could beat anybody – and he usually did. Like me he won 54 caps.

Alan Hansen enjoyed his best playing days as a member of the Liverpool side and nowadays he's a knowledgeable commentator on the game for the BBC. Alan was a natural defender, world class in fact.

Ally McCoist of Rangers, always to be relied upon to get all-important goals for Scotland.

Jock Stein had a late entry into the game but proved himself a world-class manager steering Celtic to a remarkable run of championship successes and then the European Cup. He would have surely made a hugely successful Scotland team manager had his life not been tragically cut short.

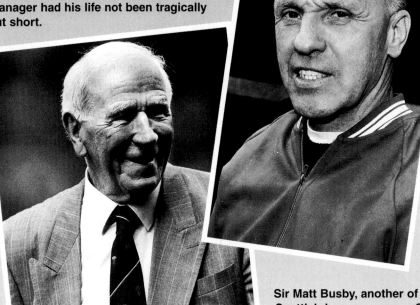

Bill Shankly was a true football genius, the man who lifted Liverpool into the top flight and then kept them there. And when he retired he left a remarkable legacy which subsequent managers could enjoy.

Sir Matt Busby, another of the great Scottish-born managers. Sir Matt did for Manchester United what Bill Shankly had done for Liverpool. With Jock Stein they formed a remarkable Scottish trio.

Wee Jimmy

THERE have been few sights in football to match the thrill of Jimmy Johnstone in full flight. The Celtic and Scotland winger was one of those players who had the crowd on their toes as soon as he got possession of the ball. Funny to think that he got all those fantastic skills by playing against lamp-posts in Glasgow.

Jimmy was born on 30 September 1944 and brought up in Uddingston, just on the outskirts of Glasgow — an area he still favours. As a kid he was like so many of us — football-mad! He explained how it all started for him.

"It began with a little rubber ball and I don't know how many pavements. I was always nuts about football and I used to dribble one of those little balls all the way to school — and all the way home again later in the afternoon. I reckoned myself as a bit of a Stanley Matthews in those days. I was really fascinated by him and his skills, and I was determined to be just like him. Even in those very young days I never considered being anything other than a winger.

"When I got home from school, I'd have my tea and then I'd be out in the street again with my ball — dribbling around the lamp-posts. Sometimes the neighbours would complain because I would keep going until ten at night — and sometimes I would get a bit too noisy as I kept up a running commentary on what I was doing. My mother would give me a real telling-off if the neighbours did complain — but she never stopped me and she really encouraged me to keep on practising."

That practice paid off as Jimmy played for the Uddingston St John's side and was spotted by Sammy Wilson, a former Celtic player. Sammy mentioned him to Jimmy McGrory who was Celtic's manager at the time. However, Jimmy Johnstone came really close to being a Manchester United player. A scout had passed on a recommendation to Matt Busby and Jimmy was given a trial.

"Sir Matt — just plain Matt as he was then — thought that Celtic had the first option on me and so, being the gentleman that he was, he stepped aside. The truth is that they had no such option, but John Higgins — a Celtic scout — soon got hold of me and I began to train at Parkhead twice a week. Since I had been a Celtic fan for as long as I could remember, I was thrilled to bits."

Jimmy's first games were with Blantyre, one of Celtic's nursery sides. He played for them for a year and was called up for his first Scottish junior cap. After that year he joined Celtic as a permanent fixture and, when he was still only 19, he made his first-team debut in a win over Clyde. It was the start of a fantastic career in senior football and made all that practice as a kid more than worthwhile.

The Jimmy Johnstone story sounds a bit like a fairy-tale, but he had his share of 'downs' as well as all the 'ups'. He was a typical red-headed, little Scot — if you don't mind me saying so. His early years at Celtic often saw him crossing swords with his opponents, with referees, and with the Celtic management. He stood less than 5ft 5ins — but he was frightened of no-one!

He seemed to settle down when he was about 26, and nobody was more relieved than his boss at Celtic, Jock Stein, who once said, "Johnstone has given me more trouble than any other player in my time at Parkhead."

Jimmy tried very hard to turn over a new leaf but it never seemed to be that simple. There are some famous stories about him. In 1967 he was supposed to be travelling down to Wembley to join us for the match against England. He never arrived. Much later we discovered that he had travelled as far as Edinburgh before deciding that he didn't feel well. He just turned round and went back home.

There was another famous occasion when he was going to Spain on holiday with his wife. They were driving to catch the ferry on the south coast of England and were then to motor through France and down into Spain. They got as far as the south coast of England when Jimmy decided that he would prefer to go to Blackpool. They spent the fortnight there instead!

Yes, Jimmy was a law unto himself all right. Another well-told story is his sailing trip. The Scotland squad was preparing for the 1974 Home International Championship and World Cup finals at Largs. Jimmy came across some unattended boats and couldn't resist the temptation of going for a row. He was dressed in a suit, which was hardly the correct sort of gear for taking a boat out to sea, but that was not his only problem. It was only after he had pushed the boat out that Jimmy realised that there was only one oar and, worse, the rowlocks were broken. The current caught the boat and away went Jimmy. He had to be rescued by the coastguard — and he got a real ticking-off from the Scottish FA.

There was never any malice in Jimmy Johnstone's actions, however — he was just high-spirited, and he still is. Not too many people know that while Jimmy was travelling all over the world with both Scotland and Celtic he was actually putting on a very brave face. The reason being that he has always had a very real fear of flying. Perhaps the word 'fear' doesn't really tell the tale. Wee Jimmy was absolutely terrified. It never stopped him from going, but for several days before and after a flight, he was far from comfortable.

Whatever his antics, Jimmy had a fantastic following among the supporters. To them he was a brilliant character who brought colour and personality to the game, but what they appreciated most was his tremendous skill. He was a master with the ball and loved to take players on, so much so that he would often beat players and then look for more to beat before he would pass the ball. It would never be a surprise to see opponents queueing to try to take the ball from him. They rarely did of course — he was not nicknamed 'Jinky' for nothing.

He was probably the most gifted player that I have ever seen in my entire life. When we played together for Scotland, I used to like to give him the ball just to watch him in action. He had tremendous skills and could send defenders the wrong way just by a twitch of the muscle. He had another amazing ability too, in that he could run like the wind with the ball and then just stop dead. I have never seen anything like it either before or since. We can all stop fairly quickly — but it takes a pace or two. Jimmy could stop dead from an all-out sprint just as if an invisible hand had pulled him back. Opponents running alongside had no chance at all.

What was also remarkable about Wee Jimmy was that he was outstanding with both feet. That is why it always surprised me that he hardly ever played in the same Scotland team as that other great little winger from Glasgow, Willie Henderson. It seems that the Scotland bosses always saw both men as right wingers, but really they could both play with both feet and Jimmy would have been more than happy to pull on the No.11 shirt as often as he was asked.

The only time that I can recall them both playing in the same Scotland side was in a 1-1 draw against Wales at Cardiff in 1966. I can't help feeling that with two great wingers like that in the side, Scotland might have fared much better in some of our World Cup adventures.

Wee Jimmy was a real 'one-off'. He was Celtic through and through and never really wanted to play for anyone else — although the prospect of him playing for Manchester United, alongside such players as Law, Best, Charlton and the others, would have been quite something had Sir Matt Busby been less of a gentleman.

Having established himself in Celtic's side, Jimmy went on to win a whole collection of medals — League champ-ionships, Scottish Cups and Scottish League Cups. His finest hour was probably winning the European Cup with his side in 1967. I have a personal memory of that because I remember watching the game on television. Remember, I was a Celtic fan myself and I was jumping around the room like everyone else that night ...but more of that later!

There was a time when I was on the park at the same time as Jimmy Johnstone and would not give him the ball to see what he could do. That was in the European Cup of the 1969-70 season, when Leeds met Celtic in the semi-final. We lost both legs 1-0 and 2-1 — and it was Jimmy that destroyed us. He was in a different class and really hurt us. Celtic lost in the Final to Feyenoord after extra time, 2-1, and I was disappointed for them because I felt that they should have won. They certainly took us apart with Wee Jimmy as their chief torturer.

On the Scotland scene, Jimmy's debut was against Wales in Cardiff on 3 October 1964. Wales won 3-2 but Jimmy did enough to secure another cap just over a fortnight later when Finland were visitors to Glasgow and were beaten 3-1. He was then rested for a few games and by the time he was recalled, I had also been given my chance and so we became team-mates.

In all, Jimmy Johnstone made 23 senior appearances for Scotland — and probably that would have doubled if he had been less of a law unto himself. Nevertheless he was a genius and, like all those who fit into that description, he had a massive personality to match that skill. George Best, Paul Gascoigne and Diego Maradona are other notable examples. You cannot fault their skill but their personalities can drive you crazy. Wee Jimmy was perhaps a little different because he was so inoffensive. You could not help but enjoy having him around.

His appearances for Scotland yielded four goals — but he

was a goal-maker rather than a goal-taker, and he was totally unselfish. Yes, he liked to beat players but he was no fool and did not try to run the ball into the net himself.

When Celtic set up that incredible run of nine successive Scottish championships from 1966 to 1974, Jimmy was involved all the way. He finally retired in 1975. Before hanging up his boots he had bought a wine-bar and dance place near his home for financial security.

I often bump into Wee Jimmy at special functions. He is kept busy with media work and personal appearances and is just as much a character now as he has always been. Next time I see him I must find out if he still takes a ball out at night to dribble around the lamp-posts!

Our Willie

WHAT would Rangers pay for a winger like Willie Henderson today? Whenever he played he generated enormous excitement and struck fear into the hearts of opponents. Willie was a tireless worker, determined to succeed and, in many ways, championed the cause of the working class of Glasgow by demonstrating that there could be life beyond the tenements.

Willie Henderson was born on 24 January 1944 in Caldercruix, a small village in the industrial heart of Lanarkshire. In Willie's boyhood days there was little else to do except work, go to the pub and play football. For kids, the pub was out of bounds and so football on the local park was the only alternative. As a result of this, Willie became one of the millions of other lads who played, talked, ate and slept football — but he proved to be one in a million by his sheer, natural talent.

A Rangers fan, he did not hesitate when a scout from Ibrox invited him for a trial. Little did he know then, that in a very short time he would not just be on the Rangers playing staff — but actually in the first team. He was simply too good to keep under wraps and, at 17, he made it into the senior side with spectacular skills that had the Ibrox fans roaring him on.

Watching Willie in action was a thrill-a-minute experience. He would launch himself along the touchline with the ball seeming to be glued to his feet. Like Wee Jimmy Johnstone he was only a little guy, and his 5ft 5ins frame was often dwarfed by the huge defenders that he had to face. But Willie had total confidence in his own ability and just left them tackling thin air as his speed and skill combined to make even the best defensive stars of the game seem like inexperienced amateurs.

However, it was not all an easy path of roses for Willie. In 1964, when he was just 20, his magic touch suddenly deserted him. The fans could not believe what they were seeing as he seemed to lose both his speed and his finesse. What none of them could realise at the time was that that Willie was in a lot of pain. People joke about bunions but it is no laughing matter when you are a professional footballer, especially one with the sort of footwork that Willie demonstrated.

It took an operation to cure the problem — and then the return to form proved to be a much slower process than the physical healing. Players like Henderson thrive on confidence and, when they hit a bad patch, that confidence takes a lot of rebuilding. There have even been instances where some players have never regained their former selves.

Willie suffered for some years. There were flashes of brilliance but he could no longer show the consistent form and talent that had made him such a big star so early in his career.

Many people said that the problem lay there — he had developed too quickly and was now a spent force. They said that so much exposure at the highest level had caused him to burn out before his mid-20s.

As well as the bunion problem, Willie seemed to get other injuries on an all too-regular basis. That also fuelled the opinion that he had been given too much to do too soon, and that he was now too fragile. An injury-prone player can go through all sorts of psychological nightmares and there were those who simply wrote him off. Even Willie himself began to wonder if he still had a future in the game.

"I was beginning to give up," he said. "I thought that I was never again going to get the touch back."

Then, suddenly, in the 1970-71 season, he was transformed back to his old self. Willie put it down to the new management set-up at Ibrox, with Jock Wallace as chief coach, that put him back on the right track.

"Big Jock made a terrific difference," Willie explained. "I used to take my outside problems into the dressing-room with me. From there I'd carry them to the training field and then, naturally, on to the field of play. Jock changed all that. He came to me just after he joined Rangers and said, "What's the problem ,wee man?" He let me know right away that he was as anxious as I was to get me back to my best.

"You've no idea what that did for me. Jock proved to be a good listener and a good counsellor. I could talk things over with him. We had a good many sessions and it did me the world of good. I found that my biggest problem was losing concentration. I was thinking too much about things that had nothing to do with the game of football. After my sessions with Jock I found that I could go into a match and just concentrate on the job in hand."

From reading this, don't get the idea that Willie was some sort of head-case. Nothing could be further from the truth. It was always said that his favourite newspaper was the *Financial Times* and, long before he retired from the game, he went into business. His business started with the opening of a hair-dressing salon in Airdrie and then, in 1970, it progressed to his opening a very successful pub in Chapelhall. He was a great believer in the personal touch, his wife Mary running the hair-dressing salon and Willie himself getting actively involved in the day-to-day running of the pub. He does not change much.

Willie Henderson also had a wicked sense of humour. He loved practical jokes and was always prepared to be on the receiving end as well as organising the 'wind-ups'.

It is understandable that while Henderson won all the domestic medals available several times over, he was disappointed that his only European medal was the runners-up award he received after defeat by Bayern Munich in the European Cup-winners' Cup Final in Nuremberg, in May 1967. Bayern won 1-0 after extra-time and the Rangers lads trooped off knowing that they had done enough to win

When Rangers reached the 1972 Final of the same competition, there were only four survivors from the 1967 game but Willie was not among them. He cheered along with the rest as Rangers beat Dynamo Moscow 3-2, but I know that he would dearly have loved to have been out there on the park that night.

As well as his medals, Willie has his Scotland caps —

some 29 of them in all. He got off to a flying start when he made his debut for his country against Wales in Cardiff on 20 October 1962. Scotland won 3-2 and Willie scored one of the Scotland goals. He was in for the next game as well and found the net again in a 5-1 win at home with Northern Ireland. Denis Law was on form for that game too — he hit the other four Scottish goals.

Willie was playing so well that he had a run of 12 consecutive internationals for Scotland. He was in the side when I made my debut in that 0-0 draw with Spain on 8 May 1965. His last appearance was in April 1971 when we lost 2-0 to Portugal in Lisbon. I missed that one, but we had been teammates on nine occasions — so I had a pretty good idea of what it was like to have him in the side.

Rangers had traditionally liked to have a certain kind of winger — the type of player who would take a direct route along the wing and put in a good cross for the big guys in the middle to head into the net. Willie was even more direct than most. He went in a straight line and made opponents get out of his way simply by conning them into thinking that he was going to go round them. His crosses were superb and if anything he was even more dangerous near goal than Jimmy Johnstone.

I still think that it was criminal that these two little giants were not given a run together in the Scottish side — especially since it would have made both sets of 'Old Firm' fans happy. As it was, when Jimmy was in the Scotland side at Hampden, there would be shouts of, "We want Henderson!", from some sections of the crowd, and then by contrast, when Willie was in the side there were calls for Johnstone from the Celtic fans.

If both players had been in the Scotland side for a run of games, not only would the crowd have cheered them both on but we would have had two of the greatest wingers in the world to terrify all-comers. I find it incredibly crazy that it never happened.

There were occasions when the two played against each other in Rangers-Celtic clashes — but they were good pals off the pitch. Willie was as much an extrovert as Jimmy but demonstrated it in a less obvious way.

Funnily enough, their careers entwined right to the end. They both played in England when they left their respective clubs and, strangely, they both headed for Sheffield. But there, once again, the great divide came into force. Jimmy joined Sheffield United in November 1975 and made 11 League appearances for the Blades that season, scoring twice.

By the time Johnstone travelled to Sheffield, Willie Henderson had already been and gone — after spending some time at the other end of town with Sheffield Wednesday. Willie played in 48 League games for the Owls and scored five goals. It seems that even during their brief careers in England, these two wonder wingers were destined to be on opposing sides — even when they were drawn to the same city.

By the time he retired, Willie Henderson had played for Scotland at schools, under-23, and senior levels and had also played for the Scottish Football League. His international career ended before the 1974 World Cup, otherwise I'm sure he would have been in the squad.

One thing that, surprisingly, Willie never won was the Scottish Footballer of the Year award. Neither did Wee Jimmy in his own right — but he was a part of that 1974 World Cup squad which I had the honour of captaining. We were undefeated and only failed to qualify from our own initial group on the minimum of goal difference. We were given a great reception when we flew back into Glasgow and the whole squad was named Footballer of the Year — so Jimmy had a share in that.

The sad thing about the retirement of such great stars as Willie and Jimmy is that they take their incredible skills with them. Willie Henderson, for example, could never teach the things that he could really do. Yes of course, he could coach the basic skills — and coach them well — but that special flair and talent could never be passed on because the players themselves do not know exactly how they do it!

To Willie, football was all about having the ball at his feet and going past other players. One of the worst — but often-asked — questions is; "What went through your mind when you did such and such?" A truthful player would answer, "I've no idea!", but most will try to oblige the interviewer by making up something that sounds about right. If you asked Henderson about a particular move he was totally unable to give you a straight answer because whatever he did was done on pure instinct. That instinct is the one ability that is impossible to teach to others. You've either got it or you haven't.

What would Rangers pay for a Willie Henderson in their side today?

Whatever was asked for him!

With their European Cup hopes frustrated year after year, the Ibrox giants know that they need a magic spell — the kind of magic you can only get from a Willie Henderson ...The Wizard of the Wing.

Alan Hansen – Better Than Beckenbauer

WHEN I look at the number of Scotland caps awarded to Alan Hansen, I am surprised. Not because he had so many — but because he was worth at least double the 26 that he actually collected. What a player! The annoying thing is that while the rest of us are gently wilting, Hansen continues to look fitter every day — and when you see him on *Match of the Day* he still looks as if he could go out and play a 90-minute Premiership game to show everyone what he is talking about.

Alan Hansen was, to me, the perfect central defender — a real world-class player who should have been in every Scotland game played throughout his career. His interest in football was through his family. They were all soccer-daft, and when 'little' Alan was born in Alloa, it was fully expected that his prime interest would be football.

They were not disappointed. Alan took to the game instantly and was soon playing for his school and district teams. One of his greatest influences was his elder brother, John, who made it into the Scotland under-23 side and played for Partick. Not too many people know that Alan could have been a Liverpool player when he was just 15. He had a four-day trial at Anfield, but the Reds did not make him an offer. In fact he almost did not come into football at all after failing to make the grade with Liverpool. Partick were happy to take him on but he did begin to consider other careers — as he explained, "During my teens I had many sporting interests and I represented Scotland at golf, squash and volley-ball. At the age of 16 I was playing golf off a handicap of two and it made me think about taking it up as a career.

"I did not think that I had a serious chance though and, with not much happening on the football scene, I took an office job with an insurance company. I had just left school, had a fair education, and I knew that I had to do something with my life. Insurance seemed to be one of those things that could guarantee you a job for life and so I embarked on my new career ...it lasted ten weeks!"

Alan did not enjoy being stuck in an office. He liked fresh air — the sort of fresh air that is unique to soccer pitches and golf courses. When Partick offered him a job as a part-time pro he didn't hesitate. He threw in the office job and lived off the part-time wages from Partick.

It seems strange now but all the time that he'd been playing the game, Hansen had been a winger. He was deceptively fast for a tall guy and he knew how to pump in a cross. Partick were sure that he had something else to offer and tried him in several other positions until finally they found the one that seemed to fit him like a glove — centre-back.

He really blossomed in that position and soon demonstrated that he was a class act. He made the Scotland under-23 side and emerged as one of the best prospects in the country. However he was still only a part-timer with Partick and he began to realise that, if he was going to make a full professional career for himself out of his obvious talents, then he was going to have to make a move.

On his senior debut for Partick he was involved in a 2-1 defeat at East Fife. It was on 27 October 1973 and was his only League game of that season. It was a bit of a step up from Sauchie Boys' Club where Partick had found him but it was as nothing compared to the fabulous football feats that he was later to achieve.

Several English clubs were reported to be interested in him after he had spent a few seasons establishing himself at Partick. Newcastle and Bolton Wanderers were among those leading the chase during that 1976-77 season, but the Jags were struggling to avoid relegation from the Premier League and the last thing that they wanted was to lose their top man. Alan had been one of the main reasons for Partick winning the First Division championship the previous season and the club now faced a dilemma. Did they keep him in an effort to avoid the drop — or should they cash in? Liverpool held the answer.

"One day I got the call to go down to Liverpool. It was near the end of the season and Partick were now safe," said Hansen. "I had heard that Liverpool had been watching me for a couple of years, but it didn't seem that they were going mad to get me to sign. When I went to Anfield to see them it became obvious that they had finally decided to take the plunge. I had no hesitation in agreeing to join them. It seemed to be the right thing to do at the right time."

Whether or not the Liverpool management team had been asked to wait until Partick were safe is a question that will probably remain unanswered. In the event, the Reds handed over £100,000 for Hansen on 6 May 1977. It was a big fee in those days although it may seem pretty insignificant now. Just three months later Liverpool sent another cheque, for four times that amount, to Scotland to obtain the signature of Mr K.M. Dalglish.

On 7 September 1977 Alan made his League debut for Liverpool in a 1-0 home win over Derby. When I tell you that the rest of the side included such players as Ray Clemence, Phil Neal, Joey Jones, Ray Kennedy, Jimmy Case, Steve Heighway, Terry McDermott, Ian Callaghan, Tommy Smith, David Fairclough and Kenny Dalglish, you can see that he was among some pretty classy performers — and that list did not include Emlyn Hughes, Phil Thompson and John Toshack who were not available on that particular day.

By the end of that first season he had made 18 League appearances, but there was much more to write home about than that. On 10 May 1978, a year and four days after signing for the Reds, Hansen's name was among those at Wembley in the European Cup Final against FC Bruges. Dalglish hit the only goal of the game and young Hansen had to pinch himself to make sure that he was not dreaming as he held his winners' medal after the match. It had been quite a debut season in England.

"I learned a lot in that first season. By becoming full-time I had had to improve my fitness and I had learned that that there was even greater chance of being punished for errors. During the European Cup Final I made a casual back-pass which could have proved costly. It made me cure any tendency to play it too coolly."

He learned quickly, eventually becoming captain of Liverpool, and remained at Anfield for the rest of his career — chalking up 620 appearances. He was still there when Kenny Dalglish left his job as manager in February 1991. There was much speculation that the greatly-respected Hansen would take over as boss, but very quickly he announced his retirement from the game before the idea started to snowball.

I do not blame him for his decision at all — but I do think that he would have made an excellent manager. He knows the game so well, he is intelligent and articulate and would have been hugely successful I am sure. As it was, Alan was was happy to call it a day after winning the European Cup three times, the FA Cup twice, the League Cup three times, the League championship eight times and, of course, the League and FA Cup double in 1986.

What of his Scotland career?

As I mentioned before, I find it almost unbelievable that Alan was awarded only 26 caps. His brother John had earned two full caps in 1972, and it was seven years later that Alan made his debut, on 19 May 1979 against Wales in Cardiff. It was a bit of a baptism of fire since Wales won 3-0, but it did not signal an abrupt end to his career. He was overlooked for the next couple of games but recalled later and then went on to play fairly regularly for his country — although not quite so regularly as many would have liked. One manager admitted that he had made a big mistake by leaving Alan out and was man enough to admit the fact publicly.

It was Alex Ferguson who admitted his error. After the shock death of the great Jock Stein as Scotland qualified for the 1986 World Cup in Mexico, Alex was handed the temporary position of manager and had to pick his squad without having too much time to watch all the players. When he named the squad, he admitted at the press conference that he felt that he had made an immediate mistake by not naming Hansen for the trip. In fairness, Alex was in a difficult situation, and it did not help that Scotland failed to get past their group games, losing to Denmark and West Germany and drawing 0-0 with Uruguay.

Alan's last game for Scotland was on 18 February 1987 against the Republic of Ireland in Glasgow. The Irish side won 1-0 and so Alan departed from the scene in the same way that he had begun — with a defeat. Through his career, however, he had enjoyed some great victories over teams like Norway, East Germany, Portugal and Sweden. He was a great international and it is worth noting that when he played in Scotland's 1982 World Cup squad in Spain, it was only goal difference that stopped them from a place in the second round. Ironically they were pipped by the USSR with whom they had drawn 2-2. It would have been fitting for Alan Hansen to have had a World Cup medal in his collection.

When Alan announced his retirement after more than 800 senior appearances, he made it clear that he was interested in taking up a media career rather than becoming embroiled in the roller-coaster ride of management and coaching. As he did with his playing career he has made a great success of it and has proved to be one of the most popular TV pundits of recent years.

For my part though, I still see him as a wonderful footballer, a cultured central defender with so many qualities that it is difficult to pick out one of outstanding strength. He had superb timing, gifted heading ability, intelligence, composure on the ball, great vision and distribution — and a wonderful understanding of the game. He didn't tackle if he didn't need to tackle — which made him a very difficult player for his opponents to shake off.

There is a lovely story about an incident during a Liverpool-Manchester United game a few seasons ago. Alan had retired a couple of seasons earlier. Graeme Souness was manager at the time. Liverpool were fighting back after being taken apart by United early on. Neil Ruddock headed a goal and whacked his head at the same time.

A few minutes later Jamie Redknapp calls across to the bench: "You'll have to sort Razor out — he's got concussion. He doesn't know what he's doing!"

Graeme Souness yelled back; "Tell him he's Alan Hansen, it might improve his game!"

That is typical of the esteem in which Alan Hansen is held. I would go as far as saying that I believe him to have been a better player than Franz Beckenbauer. I think that is the highest compliment that I can pay to one of the greatest players that I have ever seen.

Mighty Mackay

YOU have probably seen the photograph of Dave Mackay and myself having a 'discussion' during a game. The photo won a number of journalistic awards and, if you've never seen it, it shows us in a less-than-friendly pose. More of that later — let us first of all take a look at the incredible Dave Mackay who ranks very highly on my list of all-time heroes.

Sometimes I feel that Mackay was never truly given the recognition that he fully deserved. His fellow-professionals had great admiration for him — and so did the supporters of Hearts, Tottenham, Derby and Swindon. However, I don't think that the fans in general fully realised just how good he really was!

Dave Mackay was born in Edinburgh on 14 November 1934. His father worked in the printing world as a Linotype operator. Probably, Dave would have followed in his father's footsteps as so many other families did in that business —

but, his soccer talent decreed that he would be making the newspaper headlines in a very different way.

He first came into the spotlight at Wembley in 1950 when he was in the Scottish schoolboy side beaten 8-2 by England — for whom Johnny Haynes was the young star. While still a lad, he played alongside adult men for Newtowngrange Star, a local side who presented him with a souvenir watch for his performance during a season in which they won a magnificent seven trophies.

Mackay's fame spread very rapidly and before any intruder could sign him, Hearts — the team which he supported — offered him a place. It was, without doubt, one of the most important signings that Hearts ever made. It was not long before he was in the first team, looking as if he had been there for years. The trainer of those days, John Harvey, explained, "They were probably the greatest days in the history of Hearts when Dave Mackay was with us," said Harvey. "We won five trophies in the four years that he was in the first team. He played like two men — home or away. I think his outstanding quality was his competitive spirit. He never knew the meaning of the word defeat. It was a sad day for Hearts when he was sold to Tottenham but, during his first-team years, we won the League championship, the League Cup three times and the Scottish FA Cup. They were great days and there is no doubt in my mind that Dave was one of the main reasons for our success."

Who could argue with John Harvey? There is absolutely no doubt in my mind either that the Scotland schoolboy 'wonderboy' of 1950 developed into one of the greatest Scottish midfielders of all time.

Dave Mackay was fast becoming a household name in Edinburgh but the Scotland selectors did not seem to notice. They were justifiably criticised for taking so long in giving him his chance.Perhaps the selectors became a little smug after he had made his full international debut in May 1957. Scotland were taught a 4-1 lesson by Spain. Tommy Docherty was also in that Scotland side and remembers the game very vividly.

"We were murdered," he said. "The Spaniards tore us apart and only a great display in goal by Tommy Younger kept the score down. I remember how choked Dave was after we had been beaten. He had been trying to quieten the great Di Stefano — but he was having one of his really good days."

If Arsenal had not bought Mel Charles there might have been a different story to tell. Bill Nicholson, who was Tottenham manager at that time, had been thwarted in his attempts to buy Charles but he still wanted to make a significant signing and splashed out £30,000 on buying one of the best young midfielders in the game.

"We were just a good side until Dave Mackay arrived," said Cliff Jones, who played on the wing at White Hart Lane during the Tottenham glory days. "Once he had settled into that famous number six shirt we became a great side!

"He was the ball-winner. You hardly ever saw him come out of a tackle without it. Because of his enormous strength people tended to underestimate his skill yet, nine times out of ten, he would achieve something constructive once he'd gained possession."

The late Danny Blanchflower was also a Tottenham team-mate of the mighty Mackay, and once recalled his massive contribution to the great Spurs double win of 1960-61.

"It was a team effort of course, but every member of that team would point to Dave Mackay as their top player of the season. He was fantastic — not only in ability, but also in determination. He possessed a will to win that just caught you up with it. There is no doubt that he was one of the best players that I have ever seen."

Praise indeed from the great Spurs skipper who, sadly, is no longer with us.

On the domestic scene Dave Mackay fared well. He won the FA Cup three times in his ten years with Tottenham. The trophy that he really wanted was the European Cup, but in this he was thwarted — as Jimmy Greaves remembered: "Our exit from the European Cup in the 1961-62 season brought Dave the closest to tears that I've ever seen him," remembered Greaves. "This was the one he had set his heart on winning. We all had of course, but once Dave made up his mind that he wanted something then he wouldn't let anything get in his way. We were robbed against Benfica by two shocking decisions by the referee. He disallowed two perfectly good goals. Out we went and Dave was just inconsolable. That's one of the things that I'll always remember him for — his despair in defeat."

Winning meant everything to Mackay. He did not cheat but he was motivated by this great desire for success to give his all every time he pulled on a football shirt. If you asked him to take it easy he would not know what you were talking about. He was devastated by defeat but always fought back.

He was in the Scotland side that crashed 9-3 to England at Wembley in 1961. It was no consolation to him that he had been the one to score Scotland's first goal. He hated losing as

Jimmy Greaves said: "Defeat was always painful for him — but defeat by England was worse than death."

Mackay admitted that he was scarred for life by that defeat at Wembley but, as with all his scars, he was willing to carry them unflinchingly into the next battle. He was an absentee from the Scotland line-up for about two years, but he did return in time for another game against England at Wembley in 1963. This time Scotland won 2-1 and he enjoyed that rather a lot. His 22 caps yielded four goals and included memorable victories over West Germany, Norway, and each of the Home international countries.

I never played in the same Scotland side as Mackay, although we were in the same squad a few times. As I was coming in, he was going out and even being in the same training session as him was a terrific experience. It is not often that you get a pass from a legend.

Part of what made him such a hero was his recovery from broken legs. The first happened during the European Cup-winners' Cup tie against Manchester United at Old Trafford. Tottenham were 2-0 ahead after the first leg at White Hart Lane and Mackay was probably even more determined than ever — if such a thing was possible — to win, because he had missed out on a medal the previous season when injury had forced him to sit out Tottenham's triumph in the 1963 Final.

Terry Dyson was the two-goal hero of that match and he remembers how the Spurs side felt when they knew that Mackay was having to give it a miss.

"Dave was injured, and when we all realised that he wasn't going to make it to the Final we all felt as if we had been kicked in the stomach. He meant so much to the team that our morale dropped down to zero. Danny Blanchflower did a magnificent job in picking us up at a meeting of the players. In the end we beat Atletico Madrid 5-1 and I don't think that the Spanish journalists could believe it when they were told after our victory, that our best player had been sitting on the sidelines."

It is not difficult to see, therefore, why it was that Mackay was so keen to get Spurs to the Final in defence of the European Cup-winners' Cup the following season. It was not to be, however. Spurs lost to Manchester United — but that defeat was secondary to the loss of Dave Mackay, stretchered off with his leg broken.

This is where the legend really began to go into magical status. Nobody expected to see Mackay again that season but, amazingly, they did. What is even more remarkable is that his come-back was after breaking his leg a second time during a reserve match — part of his recovery schedule.

At the age of 28 it was assumed by all that Mackay would never again play at the top level. Tottenham did not expect to be able to pick him again and the national newspapers all printed tributes as if his career had died. They all reckoned without that Scottish spirit that ran through Mackay's veins instead of blood. Alan Mullery witnessed what happened during the following months at White Hart Lane.

"Sheer guts got him back," declared Mullery. "I used to see him gritting his teeth as he ran up and down the White Hart Lane terraces, pouring strength back into that left leg. It was like Everest to him. He knew that every step was taking him back toward the top of the football world. I was lost in admiration for him."

Come back he did and, in 1967, he crowned that comeback when, as captain of Tottenham, he led them to Wembley and a third FA Cup triumph. It was his last major success as a Spurs' player though. The following season he suffered a number of niggling injuries and once again it seemed that it was the end of the road for the Mackay machine. The 1967-68 season drew to a close and Tottenham announced that they were prepared to let him go for a small fee.

The obvious choice was Hearts — back home where it had all started. Manager John Harvey saw Mackay as just the player to lead Hearts back to the glory days of his previous years at Tynecastle. But then another of soccer's magical men appeared on the scene. He gained permission to talk to Mackay before any deal was signed — and talk he did ...for SEVEN hours! It was about one o'clock in the morning when that man got back into his car knowing that he had captured Mackay. Who was it? Who else but Brian Clough!

"I didn't know Dave personally before he joined Derby," said Clough. "But once he was with us he lived up to everything that I had heard about him. He was the leader that I had been seeking. His experience as captain of Hearts, Tottenham and Scotland made him the ideal general for my team of outstanding youngsters. He could only be a good influence because he had courage, dedication, ability and, above all, enthusiasm and love for the game that he had served so well. Signing Dave Mackay was the best day's work of my life."

Pre-Mackay, Derby had finished 18th in the old Second Division. At the end of the 1968-69 season they were clear winners of the Second Division championship and Mackay was joint-winner of the Footballer of the Year award, sharing it with Tony Book of Manchester City. Back in 1963, Dave had been runner-up to Stanley Matthews for this award, but now he had finally made it. I won't mention who was runner-up to him and Tony Book — I'll leave you to guess!

Mackay stayed with Derby for another two seasons, helping them to consolidate their position in the top division, before going on the move again. Swindon signed him as captain in July 1971 but, not long after he had joined them, he became player-manager. Dave did not take easily to that role at Swindon and, in October 1972, he resigned and left the club. A short spell as manager of Nottingham Forest followed but again he did not stay for very long.

In 1973 he returned to the Baseball Ground as manager of Derby County in the most difficult circumstances after Brian Clough had sensationally resigned. The Derby players — his former team-mates — told him not to come but, typical of Dave, he went anyway, won them over and during his reign, Derby won the League championship for a second time, and gave a good account of themselves in both the European Cup and the UEFA Cup as well as reaching an FA Cup semi-final. In 1976 it was time to move again. He took charge of Walsall for a year but then he realised that coaching was his strong point and so moved to the Middle East and spent nine years passing on his great experience and knowledge.

He did return in 1987 to take charge of Doncaster Rovers. I followed him there in July 1989. After that he went to Birmingham City until 1991 when he returned to coaching abroad. Off the park, Dave had an interest in a tie factory for some years. He had no complaints about how the game had treated him, although it must be said that whatever he gained from football he really earned and deserved.

Jimmy Greaves made quite a tribute to Dave Mackay when he said; "He was the greatest professional I ever played with. If ever he was missing from the Tottenham line-up, the rest of us had to work twice as hard to make up for it. We always used to say that Dave was on nodding terms with every blade of grass on the White Hart Lane pitch.

"Many a time I had reason to look up to the sky and say a silent prayer of thanks that he was with me and not against me."

As for me, I thought that Dave Mackay was quite incredible. He was like Jack Charlton and Bryan Robson rolled into one. He could do everything and he was so inspirational — ask anyone who who has ever shared a dressing-room or has played alongside him.

What was THAT photograph all about? Dave thought that I had deliberately had a go at one of his team-mates, and took exception to it. I was actually innocent but he took some convincing. I love that photo — not because of the story behind it — but because it shows me with one of my greatest heroes of all time.

Granite George

WHEN you took a look at George Young you see Rangers through and through. He was a giant of a man and you expected to see blue blood coursing through his veins, and the word 'Rangers' tattooed on his forehead. It very likely was — on the inside! It was no accident that George Young was capped 53 times by Scotland — he was simply one of the greatest defenders the old country has ever produced.

The George Young story began in Grangemouth in 1922, and when he was a teenager he played for a local side. It was almost an accident that made him a professional footballer. It began when a pal of his began training with Falkirk, not for a career in soccer but in boxing. However, George's pal enjoyed the soccer training so much that he forgot all about boxing and became a goalkeeper instead — first of all for Falkirk and then for Kirkintilloch Rob Roy, better known now as the junior club of Glasgow Rangers.

That is where George appeared on the scene. He was recommended by his pal and, after just one look, the club signed him. George was still a teenager when Rob Roy passed him on to Rangers in 1941, but he was a big guy even then. As he developed still further he was certainly an imposing sight for any opposition forward to face. He stood 6ft 3ins, and weighed in at more than 15st.

His career took off very quickly once he enlisted at Ibrox. Within 18 months he was not only a senior player with Rangers but he had made it into the Scotland team for war-time internationals. Those 53 caps that he won were for the official peacetime internationals — if you included the war-time and victory internationals as well, George actually collected a total of 75 ...and 50 of those were as captain.

George started as a full-back, but Rangers converted him to centre-half. He was not only big but he was very good in the air and not much went over his head that could not be safely scooped up by his goalkeeper. Don't get the idea that he had nothing else to offer because he was an extremely clever ball player as well. He could use both feet, beat opponents and distribute the ball expertly. George was a very skilful player.

With Willie Woodburn and Sammy Cox, Young formed what became known as the Rangers 'iron curtain'. Although George was an accomplished ball player, Rangers opted for a style which had him belting the ball out of defence into the path of onrushing team-mates. It worked too. The long ball was launched out of defence by Big George who aimed for a winger. The cross came over and there would be Jimmy Duncanson, Willie Thornton or Billy Williamson to get on the end of it.

In the post-war years from 1946 to 1957, Rangers won six championships out of a possible 11, and were runners-up in three of the other seasons. In addition, Rangers also won the Scottish Cup four times during that same period and were twice winners of the new Scottish League Cup. Those were great days for football with massive crowds. Imagine what it must have been like when Rangers beat Hibernian 3-1 in the League Cup semi-final — watched by a crowd of 125,154!

Rangers had their critics — who doesn't? However, it did not stop them from being hugely successful with their rocket attacks which were blasted off from the boots of George Young.

There was a little twist in the tail of the 1947-48 season as Rangers were eliminated from the League Cup and 'slumped' to second place in the League. It was all down to the Scottish Cup if Rangers were not to suffer the rarity of a season without a major trophy. Hibernian were again the semi-final victims in front of a massive crowd of 143,570. Morton provided the opposition in the Final and showed themselves to be no pushovers. A replay went to extra time and it looked odds-on that there would have to be a third game. Then Billy Williamson settled the matter with a late header — the only goal of the match. The two games had attracted a total of 261,151 spectators.

George Young was delighted of course and, after the game, he kept the champagne cork which became almost a lucky token for him. He took it everywhere with him and received the nickname 'Corky' on the strength of it. The following season was his best as far as domestic honours were concerned. He was at the top of his game and made a major contribution as Rangers achieved Scotland's first-ever triple-crown of championship, Scottish Cup and League Cup. He even added to his personal glory by slotting home two penalties in the 4-1 Scottish Cup victory over Clyde.

There was more drama in the 1953 Scottish Cup Final. The Light Blues had secured the League championship once again but Aberdeen were determined to stop them taking the Scottish Cup as well. A replay was needed after the initial 1-1 draw and, during the second game, Rangers' goalie George Niven was stretchered off with a head injury. As captain, George Young took the decision to go in goal himself. There were no substitutes in those days and George kept a clean sheet for 18 minutes until Niven returned wearing a rugby scrum-cap. Billy Simpson then scored the only goal of the game and 'Corky' once again received the Scottish Cup.

The 1956-57 season was significant for George. Rangers made their debut in Europe with an assault on the European Cup. They were given a bye in the preliminary round, but faced tough opposition in the first round when they were drawn against Nice. Rangers won the first leg 2-1 at home, and then lost the away leg by the same score. A third match on neutral territory saw Nice go through with a 3-1 victory.

Celtic proved to be a pain at home. They knocked the Light Blues out of both of the major cup competitions. However, the gritty Rangers men were determined not to finish the season empty-handed. They retained the League championship after it had seemed to be well out of their grasp. An unbeaten 16-match run-in did the trick and, if you doubt their determination, there was one particular game in which Rangers ran out 6-4 winners after trailing 4-1.

That championship triumph was to be George Young's last stand. He retired at the end of that season at the age of 35. He could probably have gone on for a few more seasons until he finally faded away, but he wanted to go out while the cheers were still ringing in his ears.

There was another reason why he decided to call it a day at that particular time — he was a little disillusioned. He had no problem with Rangers but he was a bit upset with the Scotland selectors.

George's international career began in wartime and so it was not until April 1946 that he made his official debut for Scotland. The game was a 0-0 draw with Northern Ireland and George played at right-back, a position that he occupied for most of his Scotland games. A year later he was in the side that drew 1-1 with England at Wembley, and so began one of the best international careers that Scotland has ever known. He missed only one of the 40 Scotland games played from the time of his first cap and enjoyed some stunning victories such as the 8-2 success over Northern Ireland in 1949, the 5-0 hammering of Belgium in 1951, the 3-0 defeat of Portugal in 1955. There were so many other notable victories as he led Scotland by example.

The upset came in 1957. Scotland were well into the qualifying stages for the World Cup of the following year and George was eagerly looking forward to that pinnacle of his career. He won his 53rd cap in a 2-1 win over Switzerland in Basle, which had come just a fortnight after a 4-2 win over Spain. To his surprise, George suddenly found himself dropped for the next Scotland game. There was no explanation — no 'thanks for everything' message. His international career was terminated as if by a shot from a gun.

He was very disappointed, of course, and that is why he decided to hang up his boots. Scotland went to Sweden without him for the 1958 World Cup finals and finished bottom of their group. George had been really keen to take part since he had also missed out on the 1954 World Cup in Switzerland when Scotland also finished up bottom of their group — especially after that painful 7-0 defeat by Uruguay. George had really wanted to do his bit for Scottish pride in Sweden — but it was not to be.

Of all his international appearances, the one that pleased him the most was against England at Wembley in 1949.

"When we came out of the tunnel my eyes caught the scoreboard with just two words on it — England and Scotland. I remember thinking, ''What's it going to say at the finish?'. I never thought about it again until a break during the second half. I looked up and it said England 0, Scotland 3. I'd seen Jimmy Mason, Billy Steel and Lawrie Reilly score their goals, but it was only when I saw the figures on that scoreboard that it really dawned on me what was happening. England did pull one back, but that final score-line of England 1, Scotland 3 has always lived vividly in my memory."

When George stopped playing he became manager of Third Lanark for a while but he was not truly happy in that kind of role. He decided to concentrate on his hotel business and restrict his soccer interests to watching and contributing an occasional piece to the newspapers.

Whenever I think of Rangers, I think of players like George Young. On the pitch he looked massive. Even as an older man he still looked magnificent and if he told you that he was making a come-back you would have little reason to doubt it.

Players of the calibre of George Young don't come along

often enough. They are unique in that you never see another player quite like them. I always believe that we should enjoy them while we've got them. There will certainly never be another George Young and the game lost one of its greatest names when he passed away in January 1997.

Hughie the Genius

HUGHIE Gallacher was a genius! Don't just take my word for it, he played long before my time anyway. Take the word of those who saw him play and those who played alongside him on the same pitch. I have seen film footage of him and, even with that limited view, there is no doubt that Hughie was one of Scotland's finest. What a tragedy it was that his life should end in such an awful manner.

But we are here to celebrate the talent of the man — a son of Scotland who began his life in Bellshill on 2 February 1903. His father, Matthew Gallacher, hailed from Northern Ireland and was a farmer. The Bellshill area was better known for its mining, but the Gallachers eked their living from the land rather than from the coal which lay beneath it.

Hughie's first competitive football was for his school team. His fame came from being one of the best centre-forwards of all time but, when he was at school, he played in goal. He was a good goalie too but, eventually during his school career, he was also given the chance to perform as an outfield player — something which he did with relish. He was used as centre-half, inside-forward and centre-forward, and he starred in whatever position he was asked to play.

One of Hughie's team-mates at school was Alex James, who himself went on to become a major force in British soccer. The two men remained friends for life and were even team-mates in the Scottish senior side.

Hughie Gallacher could not resist a game of football and he continued to play after he had left school and taken his first job in a munitions factory at Mossend. World War One was in full swing and there were many employed in keeping British soldiers fully armed. With the end of the war, Hughie was in great danger of joining the huge ranks of the unemployed, so he kept one jump ahead by going down the mines.

The tough life at the coalface hardened him considerably at a time when he was still only in his teens and not yet fully developed. In football it made him a tougher nut to crack for the many uncompromising defenders that he came to face. Be assured, he was a very clever footballer besides that growing toughness and he gave defenders a hard time in more ways than one. Not only was he difficult to take the ball from, but he was also a very aggressive player and well able to look after himself. It wasn't that he was a big guy — he wasn't. His second favourite sport was boxing and he often trained at a gym in Hamilton used by British champions, Johnny Brown and Tommy Milligan. Hughie was a pretty good fighter and could well have carved a decent career for himself inside the ropes if he had chosen to. As it was, soccer was his first love and always remained so, but those boxing skills often materialised if opposition defenders became over-zealous in their tackling. Hughie was no stranger to the early bath.

He was still only 16 when he was playing for Tannochside Athletic in junior football, which was then the hardest competition in the land. He later went to a miner's team, Harronrigg Thistle. For the uninitiated, Scottish junior football is not played exclusively by youngsters. It is junior in status but not in age restrictions and it provided young Hughie with tough adult competition.

One day he went to watch Bellshill Athletic — his local, higher-ranking, side — and by chance they happened to be a player short. He was asked to play and impressed them so much that they offered him a £10 fee to sign for them. He didn't hesitate in putting pen to paper but he never actually received the money. It was the sort of thing that was going to happen to him on more than one occasion.

Hughie's next step up the ladder came when he was 17 and had been picked to play for Junior Scotland against Junior Ireland on 29 December 1920. The game was almost over when Hughie leaped into the air to receive a cross and headed home the winner.

Queen of the South had someone watching the game and he was immediately invited to Dumfries for a trial. They discussed potential terms even before he went and a deal was struck which would earn him £6 a week — not a bad wage in those days, especially for a 17-year-old.

As his career began to take shape, so did Hughie Gallacher's problems. He fell out with his parents when they objected to him getting married at such a young age. He went ahead without their approval and became a married man but, in a very short space of time, the marriage was on the rocks. The young couple did not have a home of their own and continued to live with their respective parents, or in rooms. The marriage could not stand that sort of pressure and was about to break down completely when it was discovered that there was a baby on the way. The news held the fragile marriage together but there were further bad tidings when the baby — a son, also named Hughie — died in its first year.

The couple had a second baby — a daughter — and tried to keep their marriage from floundering, but in this they were unsuccessful and, in 1923, they parted for good. Hughie was still only 20 but his life seemed to have fallen apart. Earlier, he had been struck down by ill-health and spent some time on the danger list at Dumfries Hospital with double-pneumonia. Eventually he pulled through and then, during his convalescence, something seemed to go right for a change.

Airdrie sent a couple of directors along to see him as he recovered and offered him £9 a week to play for them. They had pulled together a good side but they knew that they needed someone a bit special to add that final touch. Hughie Gallacher was the player that they wanted and for him it was a golden opportunity to play in the top division.

He settled in during the 1921-22 season and scored seven goals in 11 League matches. The following season he hit ten goals in 18 games but it was the 1923-24 season that really announced his arrival. The upheavals of his private life had in no way damaged his natural talent for soccer and, by the end of that season, he had scored a phenomenal 33 League goals in 34 games. He also won his first cap for Scotland, on 1

March 1924 against Ireland. It was a winning debut with Scotland scoring twice without reply.

The 1924-25 season was even more remarkable with 32 goals scored in 32 League games and five more scored for Scotland in three internationals. Hughie Gallacher's fame was spreading and, early the following season, Airdrie received an enquiry from Newcastle. When the supporters heard the news they staged a demonstration — but it was to no avail. Airdrie accepted an offer of £6,500 for him and, on 8 December 1925, he ran out for the first time with his new team.

Perhaps the Newcastle fans could be forgiven for not being thrilled when they first saw him. His reputation for goals had arrived at St James's Park even before he had, and the fans were expecting to see a giant centre-forward in their colours — not this 5ft 5ins wiry Scot, who looked more likely to be of use on the wing, if anywhere. Their fears were soon dispelled, however, when they saw him at work. He scored two and made another on his debut and immediately became an adopted Geordie.

There were a few raised eyebrows when he was made captain for the 1926-27 season — but, once again, he proved his worth by leading Newcastle to the League championship. By now he was a major celebrity in Newcastle and he enjoyed every minute of it.

His social life was hectic and once again he landed himself in trouble when he struck up a relationship with the 17-year-old daughter of the landlord of one of his favourite haunts. His divorce had not yet happened and, when it was discovered that he was still married, the brother of the girl decided to demonstrate his feelings on the subject — which resulted in court appearances for both of them.

Secretly, he and the girl continued to meet and some years later, after his divorce finally came through, they married. Even that proved to be far from easy because the divorce cost Hughie £4,000 and left him penniless.

Before that, however, his success on the pitch continued and his status in Newcastle just grew and grew. He dressed well and lived up to his superstar image. In short he was irrepressible and became, perhaps, the forerunner of those 'playboy' stars of recent decades.

It came as a shock to the Newcastle supporters when they heard that Hughie was off on his travels again. It all happened in May 1930. Gallacher had just returned from helping Scotland beat France 2-0 in Paris and was taking an end-of-season break back in Bellshill. The Chelsea chairman suddenly appeared on the doorstep after the two clubs had agreed a transfer fee of £10,000. It was just left for personal terms to be arranged. Hughie played hard-to-get but terms were eventually agreed and for the next five years he became a Chelsea player.

Hughie's international career was almost over when he joined Chelsea, but he had scored 22 goals in 17 games. He played just twice more before he retired. His greatest international occasion was being a member of the famous 'Wembley Wizards' side of 1928 — but a little while later he was accused of being drunk and disorderly on the pitch during a tour of Hungary. Hughie explained that he had simply been using whiskey and water as a mouthwash and no further action was taken.

There is another enduring story about Hughie Gallacher that we cannot possibly ignore. It is the tale of Mr Fogg. Most players can tell you a hundred stories about referees but they'd have to go some to beat this one.

During November 1928, Gallacher was involved in a League match for Chelsea on a pitch that was frozen like granite. Today there would be no question of playing on such a pitch but, in those days, things were very different. Hughie was on the receiving end of some particularly fierce tackles, especially taking into account the poor conditions. When he started to hand out his own retribution, the referee asked him his name.

"If you don't know my name you've no right to be refereeing — what's your name?" snapped back Hughie. The referee was totally taken aback and simply said, "Fogg!"

"I might have guessed," responded Hughie. "You've been in a fog all afternoon."

The referee then took action, of course, and Gallacher was suspended for two months as a result. He had only been back playing for two weeks when he was called up for an international against Ireland. Guess who was refereeing? Yes …Mr Fogg! This time Hughie let his feet do his talking for him and he hit five goals as Scotland won 7-3.

But that is not the end of the story. During the 1934-35 season, Hughie Gallacher joined Derby County and in one game against Blackburn Rovers he scored another five goals. The referee was — yes, you've guessed it — Mr Fogg. Part of the transfer deal, incidentally, involved Derby paying off his debts.

Hughie played his last international during his Derby

days. He could still perform, and in 51 League games for the Rams he scored 38 goals — a record that anyone would cherish. In the summer of 1936 he moved to Notts County and was on target again, scoring 32 in 45 League games. His next move came during the 1937-38 season. He went to Grimsby and still thrilled the crowds with three goals in 11 games.

Hughie's last club saw him back in the North-East. He joined Gateshead for the 1938-39 season and there were quite a few of his former admirers from Newcastle who used to go along to watch him play. He responded as only he could — by scoring 18 goals in 31 games.

The war came along then, of course, but it is debatable whether or not Hughie Gallacher would have continued for much longer anyway. He continued to live in Gateshead but he was still dogged by an unhappy private life. Probably much of it was his own fault but we are not here to act as judge or jury. His family life was in turmoil and there were accusations that he had mistreated his daughter. He was also under suspicion of having taken illegal payments.

On 12 June 1957, when he was 54 years old, he was due in court to face a charge of ill-treatment to his daughter. He never made it to the court. Everything had become too much for him and he no longer had the outlet that playing football had given him. He felt like yesterday's hero and, on the night before his court appearance, he walked in front of an express train. It is said that just as he stepped forward, he lightly bumped against a bystander and the last word that he ever uttered was, "Sorry!"

When I was manager of Doncaster Rovers, I often had a

cup of tea with Jackie Bestall who had played alongside the great man. He enthralled me with the stories of his skill and it would seem that, if anything, Hughie was even more brilliant than anyone actually realised. He was unbeatable in a one-against-one situation.

Put in simple terms, Hugh Kilpatrick Gallacher was a true Scottish soccer genius.

Alex Young –The Golden Vision

FATHERS and grandfathers speak about Alex Young in hushed tones when they tell younger Everton fans about the fantastic former Goodison star for whom the word 'hero' is just much too small. Goodison Park echoed to the shout, "Alex Young ...Alex Young ... " for much of every match — and he rarely failed to respond. He was a unique player with a style that was almost exclusively his own.

Alex Young was born in Loanhead on 3 February 1937. He shone in schoolboy soccer and was soon snapped up by Hearts. It did not take long for him to make the first team as everyone who saw him was totally smitten by his amazing ability on the ball. He was a centre-forward but unlike any other at that time. He was not the usual big, burly, bustling, giant No.9

favoured by most sides as a target man for crosses. He played in a much deeper role, almost like an attacking midfielder, and would take on players, keep possession, and then score.

When he left school, Alex had taken a job as an apprentice mining engineer. The prospect of becoming one of the biggest soccer stars of his age never even occurred to him. However, he enjoyed every minute of his football and did not hesitate when the opportunity to play the game professionally presented itself.

Hearts were responsible for him becoming a centre-forward. He had begun life as a winger, but showed an eagerness to stray inside and get within shooting range. That's what gave them the idea of trying him in a more central attacking role. It was quite a formidable Hearts side in the late 1950s when Alex was playing. The line-up included Dave Mackay, John Cumming, Willie Bauld, Jimmy Wardhaugh, Alfie Conn, Ian Crawford and Jimmy Murray. No wonder that they had such a good spell.

In 1958, Hearts won their first Scottish championship of the season and they did it in style. Murray, Wardhaugh and Alex Young scored 80 goals between them in the title race — Alex getting 24 of them. At the end of that amazing 1957-58 season, Hearts had dropped only six points throughout the season. Their 34 games resulted in 29 victories, four draws and only one defeat. Finishing on 62 points they were 13 points clear of Rangers — the runners-up. Remember that this was at a time when there were two points for a draw. Impressed? Well, how about this? In those 34 League games they conceded only 29 goals and scored a massive 132! That's an average of almost four goals per game!

Alex Young was still at the club two years later when Hearts repeated their performance and became champions again. This time they only managed 102 goals, just three goals per game. It was obvious by now that Young's days at Hearts were numbered. Dave Mackay had already gone to Tottenham and other English clubs were casting envious eyes north of the border. They could not fail to notice the blond bundle of talent that was Alex Young.

Everton finally took the initiative in November 1960 when manager John Carey saw him as just the player to add both fire and goal power to his rebuilt side. Carey had been in charge at Everton since the latter part of 1958. He had taken over a team in trouble — at the foot of the old First Division and still reeling from a 10-4 defeat by Spurs. The club had been in turmoil for a number of years and Carey came in as the manager who could not only calm that turbulence, but also put Everton back on the path to success.

Johnny Carey was a very good manager and he recognised a star player when he saw one. He willingly paid around £30,000 for Alex Young and it was to prove to be a master signing. No other Everton player — not even Alan Ball, Howard Kendall, Neville Southall or Duncan Ferguson — has ever captured the hearts of the Goodison faithful quite like Alex Young.

It had been years since they had experienced the excitement that he generated whenever he had the ball. Whenever he received it there seemed to be a goal in the air. He would get the ball, throw down a challenge to absolutely anyone who stood between himself and the goal and, after beating whoever picked up the gauntlet, he would fire in a shot that only the best were able to handle. The Evertonians loved it.

His Everton career lasted from November 1960 until May 1967 and he scored 77 League goals in 228 games. He also made countless others by unselfishly slipping the ball to a team-mate when he might well have sealed the glory for himself. During his days at Goodison his side won the FA Cup in a 1966 Final that was one of the best ever seen at Wembley Stadium. But for that other game that took place in the same stadium a few weeks later, when England beat West Germany, this game would have been shown over and over again.

Jim McCalliog was in the Wednesday camp while Alex Young was his counterpart for Everton. The fire of these two Scots raged through all 22 players to create a match that was a brilliant advertisement for British soccer. In the end it was that extra buzz and sharpness from Alex Young that won the day and, of course, the FA Cup.

That was not the only medal that Alex won with Everton. There was great rejoicing among the blue-clad Merseysiders in 1963 when the League championship was presented to the Goodison club. They finished six points clear of Tottenham and 17 points clear of rivals Liverpool — there were big grins all round Goodison that summer.

In 1967 Alex Young left Everton. He was now aged 30 and beginning to feel the effects of all those tackles — but he did not give up. He signed for Glentoran and spent the next year and a bit wowing the fans in the Irish League. Needless to say, his new side were champions at the end of that season.

Alex was not finished with English football just yet, however. In November 1968 he was signed by Stockport County for £16,000. It was to be his last season. Another ankle injury meant that he struggled to maintain fitness throughout the campaign and made only 23 appearances. He scored five times and Stockport finished in improved, but unheralded, ninth place. He decided then to hang up his boots.

Alex Young's Scotland career began in the under-23 side. He also played for the Scottish League during his Hearts days and you would think that he would have won enough Scottish senior caps to fill a cupboard or two. In fact he was capped only eight times.

His senior debut was on 9 April 1960 at Hampden. England were the visitors and Alex Young took his place alongside Ian St John and Denis Law. Dave Mackay was also in the side so he was in good company. The result was a 1-1 draw and Alex was not picked again until two months later when Scotland were away to Hungary and drew 3-3 in a thriller. This time Alex scored and was kept in the side for the next game three days later. This was away to Turkey who won 4-2 — but Alex was on the scoresheet again.

The seventh international in which Alex Young played was against the Republic of Ireland in Dublin on 7 May 1961. He put on an incredible performance, scored twice and engineered a 3-0 victory that was a tribute to Scottish football. He was then dropped!

Five years later he was selected again and played part of a game against Portugal which resulted in a 1-0 defeat at Hampden. That was the end of Alex Young's international career. What happened between May 1961 and June 1966 is a mystery about which only the powers-that-be have any answer. I was in the side for his last appearance and I promise you that he was as brilliant as ever and was also as keen as ever to be playing for his country.

It is a good job that the men who took the decision to drop him did not live on Merseyside. The Everton fans would have demonstrated how they felt about it just as they did in 1966 when Alex was inexplicably dropped from the Everton first team for a game or two. Harry Catterick was the manager then and , in February 1966, he decided to drop Alex in favour of a 16-year-old boy by the name of Joe Royle (I wonder what happened to him?). Everton fans were stunned and some of them even showed their disgust by physically attacking poor Harry outside Blackpool's ground where Everton had been playing. That is a measure of how much a hero Alex had become at Goodison Park.

Alex himself took it all in his stride. He enjoyed his football and he enjoyed being a professional, but he never allowed himself to get carried away with all the incredible hero-worship. He was even described as the 'Scottish Di Stefano', but he shrugged that off too.

"Alfredo Di Stefano was one of the greatest players ever to wear a No.9 shirt. I was flattered to be even mentioned in the same breath," said Alex. "I never tried to model myself on him, but there were times when his style suited me for some occasions. He had a fabulous football brain and adapted to each game — sometimes playing a straight centre-forward, other times dropping right back to defence and bringing the ball forward from a very deep position. I'm no Di Stefano, but I liked to think that what was good enough for him and Real Madrid was good enough for me and whatever team I was with.

"At Everton I had a fine understanding with my team-mates. It didn't matter who scored the goals just as long as they were scored. If I could not shake off an opponent, then I would take him with me and create a gap for someone else. The simple way is always the most effective way — but you have to use your brains instead of brawn, to decide which is the simple way."

When Alex decided to call it a day, soccer lost a great player. He pursued other interests outside the game and, in my opinion, that was a great pity because not only did he possess tremendous talent but he also had a great brain with fantastic vision. He would have been a great manager or coach.

Instead he has become a memory — but what an incredible memory ...Alex Young, the Golden Vision.

Caesar McNeill

BILLY MCNEILL — the Celtic colossus, or Caesar as he was sometimes called — was a real giant of a player. It was not that he was seven feet tall, but somehow he always looked to be a colossal man — especially with his arms aloft, holding a trophy.

As a player, Billy was very, very special. Not only was he a great player but he was always so inspiring — the sort of man who would run through a minefield and everyone would follow him without the slightest hesitation. He just inspired comradeship and was the kingpin of that great Celtic side of the 1960s.

McNeill's background was very typical. Brought up as a Celtic fan in Glasgow, there was nothing more to life than kicking a football from dawn until dusk and cheering on those green and white hoops. Perhaps you have to be a Glaswegian to fully understand it, but the city and its people are dominated by the game, probably more than any other city in Britain. I have known players who have been involved with Glasgow derbies and also derbies on Merseyside, in Manchester, London, the Midlands and the North-East, but they all say the same thing — there is nothing to touch the rivalry and the football fever of Glasgow.

Billy McNeill was brought up in just that kind of environment. He was born in Bellshill on 2 March 1940 and, like most of us, he played football from the time that he was able to stand up on his own two feet. He played for his school and then the local boys clubs until one day his dream came true and he was invited to Celtic.

It was not long before he made his first-team debut, and so began an incredible senior playing career that did not end until 1975, when he finally decided to quit while he was still at the top. During his years at Celtic, he played no fewer then 790 competitive first-team games — which is quite a record. His 486 League appearances for the Bhoys is still a club record.

When you add his international appearances, you can see that we are talking about a truly outstanding player who performed at the very top of his profession in more than 800 senior matches, most of which were, what you might call, 'pressure' games. There was nowhere to hide for Billy McNeill — and if there had been he would have rejected it.

Billy always paid tribute to the man who had been the greatest influence on his career — Jock Stein! ...Who else? When Billy first joined Celtic, Jock was club coach with particular emphasis on the reserve and youth sides. Billy and Pat Crerand were among the stars he recruited during the late

1950s and, by the time the Big Man had been appointed Celtic manager in March 1965, McNeill had certainly blossomed into a terrific player.

Billy never forgot the treatment he received as a lad from Jock Stein and, when he became one of the club's senior statesmen, he helped other youngsters to settle in at Parkhead. One such youngster was a lad by the name of Kenny Dalglish, you may possibly have heard of him.

The qualities that McNeill demonstrated in his play showed that he would be a perfect choice as captain, and it was one of his proudest moments when he led his team out for the first time. He was not short of other memorable moments either as his huge medal collection proves.

Billy was one of only three players to win seven Scottish Cup winners' medals when he played a major part in Celtic's victories of 1965, 1967, 1969, 1971, 1972, 1974 and 1975, a terrific achievement. He also won five Scottish League Cup winners' medals and no fewer than nine Scottish championship medals. There was also that famous night in Lisbon in 1967 when Celtic conquered Europe — but more of that later.

Billy McNeill was held in great esteem by the press, public and players alike. He still is, of course. Perhaps two of his greatest accolades were that, in 1965, he became the first Scottish Footballer of the Year (elected by the Scottish Football Writers' Association) and, in 1974, he went to Buckingham Palace where the Queen invested him with the MBE in recognition of his great service to the game of football.

His other honours included playing for his country. Billy's

first cap came in 1961 on an ill-fated day for Scotland. The game was against England at Wembley on 15 April in that year and, yes, it was THAT one. England won 9-3, despite an all-star Scottish line-up which included Dave Mackay, Eric Caldow, Denis Law, Ian St John and others of top calibre. It must have been a terrible shock to Billy McNeill to trudge off the pitch after his international debut, knowing that his side had just suffered a defeat that would go down in history

He was made of stern stuff, however, and was there in the line-up for Scotland's next game which was a 4-1 win over the Republic of Ireland in Glasgow. A few days later he was in the side for the return match in Dublin which Scotland again won — this time 3-0.

Billy was in the Scotland side when I made my debut in May 1965 against Spain at Hampden. He was one of my prime motivators that day and helped me to keep calm and confident on my first big day which resulted in a 0-0 draw. We were both in the side when he signed off as an international. It was on 27 May 1975 and against England at Hampden. Billy really wanted to win that one, but England emerged as the victors with the only goal of the match. His games against England were not all defeats however — there were two victories and some drawn games as well. There were other triumphant experiences among his 29 caps as well, and he even found time to put three goals away — including one in a bizarre 8-0 win over Cyprus.

When Billy McNeill decided to retire from the game in 1975, he was not lost to football, but decided to opt for management and coaching. He became boss of Aberdeen for a while before Alex Ferguson, but it was only a matter of time before he returned to Parkhead becoming, once again, the inspiration in the home dressing-room — this time as manager. He followed in the footsteps of his friend and mentor, Jock Stein.

Under Billy's guidance, Celtic won the championship in 1979, 1981 and 1982, and took the Scottish Cup in 1980. Celtic were faring well with Billy at the helm. Unfortunately, there was a falling-out between him and the board over a difference of opinion regarding his salary. As a result, he left and became manager of Manchester City. Life was not the same for Billy in England, however, and, in just under four years at Maine Road he could not find the formula for success. He left there in 1987 and had a short spell as boss of Aston Villa before returning to Scotland and a second crack at Celtic.

Times had changed at Parkhead and Billy could not get things going as he had before. Eventually he parted company with the club once again in June 1991 — and that signalled a change of direction for him. He became a media pundit with regular appearances on BBC television and also continued to run his pub — the two time-consuming passions that are still keeping him busy today.

Anyone who ever saw Billy in action could never forget him. I played alongside him and I played against him, and from whichever angle he was an awesome footballer. Another team-mate, Celtic's Bobby Murdoch said, "Billy McNeill sets a high standard of conduct for us all — and this is the main reason you do not see any long-haired wonders walking through the doors at Celtic Park as playing-staff members of the club. Professional football is our business. We feel that we do not have to look like a crowd of discotheque drop-outs to attract attention."

That was part of the appeal of Billy McNeill. It was not just that he was a world-class footballer, but that he was such a good example to other professionals. It was not what he said, it was what he was. He never claimed to be a soccer genius but he was so obviously outstanding nevertheless — solid in defence, and a major threat at the other end whenever Celtic earned a corner.

My former Leeds pals, Mick Jones and Allan Clarke, both described him as their most difficult opponent. He rarely described himself but once gave us a little insight when he said, "Angels don't win you anything except a place in heaven! Football teams need one or two vagabonds."

It was Billy's way of saying that he was a rough-and-ready sort of player — rugged, but never dirty or a cheat. He was the kingpin of the great Celtic side of the 1960s and early 1970s. His very last game for Celtic was the 1975 Scottish Cup Final in which he once again played with his heart on his sleeve. Airdrie were the victims as Celtic won 3-1 and there was the final picture of him with yet another medal in his hand and the trophy raised up above his head.

Billy McNeill always believed that Glasgow itself played a major part in his career and his passion for the game.

"You have only to be in Glasgow on the day of a major game to feel the excitement and tension in the air — to know that this is THE DAY for so many people in this great city. Glasgow is legendary as a soccer-mad city and that passion gets into you and becomes a part of you. The only way to really get that feeling out into the open is to play football."

Billy certainly lived up to his own words. There was never any doubt that his play reflected his great love and feeling for the game and his total commitment to Celtic and to Scotland.

I see Billy McNeill now and then, and he still shows that very special drive for the game. That probably comes over in his television and radio appearances. There is something else as well. Here is a man who has been to the top of the mountain. He has been honoured and revered by the best and yet it has never changed him. He always was — and still is — essentially a very nice chap who just loves football.

For me, whenever I think of him, I see this colossal man holding aloft the European Cup.

Danny Boy

W HEN Danny McGrain became manager of Arbroath a couple of years ago there was a rush to buy false beards and, at the very first home game, the fans welcomed him by sporting those beards to show their approval. In short, Danny had become a cult figure in Arbroath overnight. But all of that was nothing new to Danny — although his cult following as a Celtic star had taken a little longer.

Many people will tell you that, during his time, Danny McGrain was the best right-back in the world. I would not argue with that. We were in the 1974 World Cup squad together and, believe me, he took some beating. He would have been at home in any team in the world — which made it all the more reassuring to know that he was wearing a Scotland shirt.

Danny was born in Glasgow on 1 May 1950. He went through all the usual stages of schools soccer and was quite well-known in those circles by the time he had reached his teens. It was not long, therefore, before he was noticed and snapped up by one of the two Glasgow giants. At the same time that Danny joined Celtic, another young man was also signed — Kenny Dalglish. They knew each other from schools soccer and became good pals — a friendship that has lasted down to this day. It was not just that they happened to join together — but that they were both Rangers fans!

Danny's career had developed steadily through the stages of youth and reserve football until he made it into the first team. From the moment that he had joined Celtic he was dedicated to Parkhead. His favourites, Rangers, had made an approach early on, but he appreciated that it was Celtic who had made the first move and so he remained loyal to them throughout his playing career.

It says a great deal for Danny's resilience and tenacity that, not long after making his name in the first team, he had to overcome an injury that would have put many footballers out of the game for good.

He was a few months short of his 22nd birthday when, in February 1972, he suffered a serious head injury while playing against Falkirk. It proved to be a fractured skull and even Danny realised that it was a career-threatening injury — as he explained in an interview a few years later.

"During the time that I was laid aside, there were moments when I wondered whether I'd make it. Then, when I thought about having to go out and work at something other than football to make a living, I buckled down to make sure that I'd be playing again."

When Danny first got into the Celtic senior team he had to overcome the challenge of getting selected in favour of such established stars as Tommy Gemmell, Jim Craig and

Davie Hay. There was no way that he was going to let something like a fractured skull keep him out of the side. He was soon back on top form and even better. Perhaps having come so close to seeing his dream shattered gave him an extra edge.

His manager, the great Jock Stein, paid tribute to him.

"Danny's professional in everything," said Jock. "He's a bit of a dream player — never any trouble. He just works away at the game. He came to us as a wing-half but we juggled him about a bit. That was our policy. We discovered that he was probably best at full-back. I think he has proved us right."

He certainly did. He was a great attacking full-back. He was fast, could beat opponents and get crosses into the box that caused havoc. For me, it was his tackling that made him such a great player. Everyone talks about him being an outstanding player going forward — but they seem to forget about his ability to tackle. He had perfect timing, great courage and a gift for ball-winning that is rarely seen with such class today. He was never a dirty player — he never needed to be.

Danny McGrain was not only an excellent club player, he also starred for his country. His Scotland debut was in 1973 against Wales in Wrexham. I actually missed the game, but Danny had a great debut as the Welsh were beaten 2-0 with George Graham scoring both our goals. It was the start of a long Scotland career for Danny and I'm proud to say that we were team-mates on a number of occasions.

When we went to West Germany for the 1974 World Cup finals, Danny McGrain played in each of our three group games and, like the rest of us, was disappointed when we had to come home empty-handed — even though we were unbeaten. In the competition, Danny was one of our best players and thoroughly deserved his share of the praise bestowed upon the squad that year.

Not long after that 1974 World Cup he sustained a nasty ankle injury but, again, did not sit on the sidelines for long. Danny fought his way back and, although I suspect that he carried that injury for the rest of his playing career, he never let it show or affect his play. He bounced back to further international acclaim and, after missing the 1978 World Cup finals, he was there in 1982 when Scotland went to Spain for the tournament and played in the 5-2 win over New Zealand.

Danny captained the side that day in Malaga, at the same time winning his 62nd, and final, cap. It was a great farewell. He had begun his international career with a victory, and he finished it in style with another terrific win.

Danny's picture is in the Hall of Fame at the Scottish Football Association headquarters in Glasgow, a fitting tribute to an outstanding international player.

That was by no means the end of his playing career. Danny continued to be a regular first-choice defender for Celtic until the end of the 1986-87 season when he finally decided to call it a day.

Danny's playing career had won him a great collection of medals, including seven championships, five Scottish Cups and two Scottish League Cups. In 1977 he was Scottish Foot-baller of the Year, but probably his favourite medal is the MBE he received for his services to football.

"My biggest disappointments were, not playing in the 1978 World Cup, and playing in four losing League Cup Finals. I can hardly believe that we lost that many times at the final hurdle."

There was another disappointment for Danny when he became manager of Arbroath in 1992. His presence had an immediate effect — at least among the fans. A wave of optimism swept through the club but, without a sudden — and large — investment of cash, clubs like Arbroath will never, realistically, compete for any length of time against the big boys of the Premier League.

Danny enjoyed the experience of managing Arbroath, even though it lasted no longer than a season. He liked being in the backbone of Scottish soccer — for that is surely what clubs like Arbroath are all about.

"It was good to be close to the game and close to the supporters as well. The attendances might well be measured in tens of hundreds rather than tens of thousands, but that doesn't matter. It's the game that counts and not how many people are watching it. I found Arbroath to be a friendly club in a friendly area. The supporters were brilliant and I was very flattered when they all started wearing false beards."

Danny McGrain has always been a clean-living family man. His family have always meant more to him than anything else. Perhaps that is why he has never rushed to take on a management role.

It is hard work, with long gruelling hours and a lot of travelling. The sort of job in which you have to carry family photographs with you — just to remind you of what they look like.

He still gets involved with coaching and, of course, he is always in demand for personal appearances and media work. His public still want him and even Rangers fans admit that Danny McGrain is much more than just a former footballer.

He is a national institution with his rough-and-ready determination to do well.

It was a long trek from Maryhill Juniors to the top of his profession but Danny McGrain earned his success. When he gave up the captaincy of Celtic, near the end of his playing career, it was Roy Aitken who took over and filled a vacancy that had left a mighty gap in the Celtic side.

"Danny *was* Celtic," said Roy. "I knew that he was going to be almost impossible to follow. He was an excellent player and the fans thought the world of him. He was sorely missed by everyone."

There is no doubt about that. Probably the greatest compliment paid to Danny McGrain was one that was often paid by opposing managers. Such was Danny's attacking flair that managers of the opposition used to get their wingers to mark him. It is not often that a defender is marked by an opposing forward.

Danny made more than 400 League appearances for Celtic and, as we have already mentioned, his attacking flair, coupled with his undoubted skills as a defender, made him one of the greatest players in Scottish soccer history. Amazingly, it was an extreme rarity for him to actually score and in 20 years at Parkhead he netted only five League goals.

"I was never a goal-scorer," said Danny. "I could stop them at our end and lay it on for someone else to score at the other end — but I was definitely not a goal-scorer myself. For me, putting the ball across for someone else to nod home was as good as scoring myself."

His lack of goals did not stop him from becoming Celtic's most-capped player of all time. It did not stop him from having an outstanding career for both club and country. Perhaps more than that, it did not stop him from being one of the best-loved players that Scotland has ever known.

Despite all its drawbacks, I sincerely hope that he has not been put off club management for ever. It would be a great loss to Scottish soccer if he never made any further contribution. After all, there is only one Danny McGrain.

Super Ally

I T IS impossible to be in the company of Ally McCoist for more than a few minutes without having a huge grin spread across your face — he is just that kind of a guy, both on and off the pitch. The big difference between the match and the rest of his time is that during that 90 minutes, Ally McCoist can be a heart-breaker — one of the most lethal goal-scorers that Scotland has ever produced. I can only really describe Ally as very, very special.

Amazingly for such a superstar, his story had such simple beginnings. He was born in Bellshill and named Alistair Murdoch McCoist — and you cannot get much more Scottish than that. At school he was an impish player who just could not stop scoring goals. He did not neglect his education though and gained eight passes in a variety of subjects at 'O' level, and then went on to higher honours in both English and Chemistry. Personally, I would not allow him within a hundred miles of a chemistry set — anything could happen!

Although he worked hard at school, football was rarely out of his mind. He loved to play and he was also a very keen Rangers fan and dreamed of one day being able to pull on the famous shirt.

As it happened, Ally was indeed spotted by a talent scout while he was playing for the famous Firs Park Boys' Club. Before long he was signing on the dotted line — but not for his beloved Rangers! It was St Johnstone who had captured him.

"They did a lot for me at St Johnstone," said Ally. "Including giving me my debut. I made the Scotland youth team as well, so I have a lot to thank them for."

That first-team debut was on 7 April 1979, and was marked by a 3-0 win over Raith Rovers. McCoist was only 16 at the time. His senior debut was the start of a three-season run which saw him score 22 goals in 57 matches, before St Johnstone accepted a £400,000 bid for him from Sunderland, which took him to Roker Park for the 1981-82 season.

For a while it seemed as if the McCoist machine had run out of steam as he scored only a handful of goals in a couple of seasons of fairly regular first-team football. He later explained that, while he thought a lot of Sunderland and the club's great supporters, he missed Scotland a lot and it affected his form.

Ally's dream finally came true when Rangers expressed an interest, and he signed for them in the summer of 1983. Rangers themselves perhaps didn't realise just how much of a bargain they were getting when they handed over £185,000 to Sunderland. It must have been one of the snips of the century. Jock Wallace was the man who signed him for Rangers, and he saw in McCoist a talent that was not only to take Scotland by storm, but Europe as well , when he emerged as one of the game's sharpest finishers.

"I was joint top scorer in my first season at Rangers," remembered McCoist. "I played in 30 League matches and scored nine goals. I was growing in confidence all the time as the Rangers coaching worked on me."

It certainly did work on him. He hit a goal streak that has only ever been thwarted by injury, and he has one of the greatest strike rates in the game with something like 50 per cent success on goal attempts. When you analyse that it is phenomenal. It is no wonder that he has been the top scorer at Ibrox every season since he joined except for those times when he has been irregular in the team through no fault of his own.

When you start to look at his various scoring feats and records, it is quite mind-blowing. Just picking out a few examples: in the 1985-86 season he scored 24 League goals in 33 games; the following season it was 33 in 44 games; the 1987-88 season saw him hit 31 in 40 League games. It didn't stop there. Some began to write him off when he fell out of favour with manager Graeme Souness — but Ally bounced back in style. The 1991-92 season ended with a remarkable tally of 34 goals in 38 League games, and the following season he hit another 34 goals in just 34 games ...amazing!

I have never been a statistics buff but you cannot ignore figures like that. Ally McCoist is simply the greatest goal-scorer in the Scottish Premier League and — for my money — in Britain. He holds the record for Premier League goals and every time he scores one he extends his own record again.

What makes him so special? He is an opportunist — the sort of player who may be tightly marked throughout a game but will still make that sudden turn which loses his guards and put him into a scoring opportunity. He is an escapologist, capable of squirming away from even the closest attendance. He is not just nuisance-value, he is a hit-man, a quick-draw specialist, brilliantly capable of materialising in the right place at the right time to break the hearts of the sternest defenders and to score golden goals.

When McCoist scored against Motherwell in a 3-0 win in December 1989, he put himself into the history books again by scoring Rangers' 7,000th League goal. And there were even more records to tumble. He broke the club scoring record a few years ago and is still breaking it. A goal against Falkirk in December 1992 meant that he became the first Premier League player to hit 200 goals in that competition. Who is to say that he won't make it 300 before he has finished?

His scoring feats have earned him acclaim overseas too. In 1992 he won the Golden Boot as the top league scorer in Europe. He was thrilled to win that, as he explained at the time.

"It meant a lot to me to win that. Scoring goals for Rangers means that I am doing my job and paying back the faith that the club put in me. Winning the Golden Boot award meant that I had also done something for   Scotland — especially when you look at all the great names who have won it previously."

Among those names is Marco Van Basten, one of the deadliest strikers in the game — and McCoist's hero.

"Marco was one of the most complete strikers of the lot, and if I thought I could play even half as well then I would be happy."

Then Ally went on to declare an ambition that was to prove to be quite prophetic.

"I haven't finished with the Golden Boot yet. My ambition is to win it twice. If all goes well I hope to be among the challengers again — and if I can win it for a second time and make it a double for Rangers and Scotland, that would be fantastic."

The very next season he did just that. It was an achievement to be proud of. There was every chance that Ally would make it three in a row, until he was struck down by a potentially career-ending injury while on international duty.

Ally McCoist began his international career in the youth side as we have mentioned. Later he was selected for the under-21 side to play Belgium in 1984. His senior debut came on 29 April 1986, and it was a real baptism of fire since Scotland were playing away to Holland. The Scots won a moral victory by coming away with a goalless draw — and Ally played his part by keeping the Dutch defenders busy.

It was the start of a great international career that has also seen him enter the Hall of Fame at the SFA headquarters. McCoist kept his place in the Scotland side but he had an uncharacteristic problem in getting the ball into the net during those early games of his international career. He finally announced his arrival on 9 September 1987 when making his seventh appearance for Scotland. Hungary were the visitors to Hampden and Ally scored the only two goals of the game to take his country to a memorable victory.

He has scored many Scotland goals since of course. One of the most important was against Norway at Hampden in 1989. It clinched Scotland's place in the 1990 World Cup. Ally has played for Scotland in both World Cup and European championship tournaments and he has a proud international record with a place among the top four Scotland scorers of all time. However, it was in a Scotland shirt that his career nearly ended.

In 1993, Scotland were playing Portugal in a World Cup qualifier in Lisbon. To put it mildly, it was a tough game which ended with the Scots going down 5-0. The result became of secondary importance however as the prime concern was for McCoist who had been felled in a tackle and did not get up. His leg was badly broken, and thus began a 27-month injury spell that would have had many of us throwing in the towel ...but not Ally McCoist!

"I would have hated my last international appearance to be a 5-0 defeat, with a broken leg to remember it by. I was determined then to get back into the side one day and that determination did not diminish — even though it was a tough road back with plenty of set-backs.

"It was frustrating not to be involved with Scotland, but it would have been much more soul-destroying if it had been the same injury all the time. It started with the broken leg but along the way, the so-called road to recovery, I picked up an ankle problem, a hernia, two different torn muscles and various other twinges. I definitely struck Portugal off my holiday list!"

Through all of that, Ally McCoist gritted his teeth and smiled his way through the pain barrier. It was tremendous to see him back in the side as a substitute when Scotland took on Greece in August 1995, in a European championship qualifier. The plot could not have been arranged better by a fiction writer. Ally McCoist sits fidgeting on the bench, watching his team-mates struggle to break down a solid Greek defence. Craig Brown tells him to warm up. There are 20 minutes left and he is sent on. Sixty seconds later Hampden erupted as John Collins crosses and Ally's flashing header beats the clawing keeper. It was real 'Roy of the Rovers' stuff.

The Scotland goals have continued to stack up for McCoist. He scored in the European championship tournament in England last year and it would come as no surprise to me if he was in France to take part in the 1998 World Cup tournament.

Few honours have escaped Ally during his career. In addition to his great collection of caps and those Golden Boots, he was also Scottish Footballer of the Year and Scottish PFA Player of the Year in 1992. He has won an incredible number of Player of the Month, Goal of the Month and Man of the Match awards. Then, of course, there is a whole list of medals that he has won with Rangers.

Since he joined the Ibrox club he has collected no fewer than nine Scottish championship medals. By the time that this book appears on the shelves he might well have added another — or even improved on his tally of Scottish Cup and Scottish League Cup medals.

Where will it all end? Knowing him, it is quite likely that he will wake up one morning and just decide to call it a day. It will be a great loss to Scottish football when that day arrives. I believe that the Scotland team would certainly have suffered if he had not fought his way back from injury. Rangers, too, would have found him incredibly difficult to replace — perhaps impossible. It is not just his fantastic ability to score goals, but his tremendous personality. He is a great little guy who bubbles all the time and destroys tension.

For the moment it seems that Ally is determined to keep playing, even though he so obviously has a great full-time career awaiting him in the media. He still has some soccer ambitions at the back of his mind.

"At the end of the day it is up to others to decide whether I am good enough or fit enough to play. But I certainly feel that I'm fit enough to be playing at the top level well into the next century. I have always said that I want to be in the Rangers side that plays against Celtic on New Year's Day

2000, but I feel well enough to look beyond that. I had a testimonial a few years back and I reckon that I'm due another one in 2003, so I wouldn't mind to stay in the first team until then — at least!"

Nobody would bet against him doing just that. There has been talk of him going to play in Japan before he finally hangs up his boots, and no doubt he could earn big money for a season or two out there. I've got a feeling though, that when Ally does blow the final whistle on his playing career, it will be sudden and it will be for keeps.

He does not take himself seriously and I think he will make a clean break from the playing side of the game rather than watch his appearances dwindle and his goals gradually dry up. I doubt that he will go into management because he is not the sort of guy who could tolerate that sort of hassle. He will continue to beam at us from our television screens for years to come and I personally welcome that. His personality is like a breath of fresh air. You will never hear anyone say a bad word about him.

It's an old, used and abused expression that someone is 'a legend in his own lifetime', and yet it would be true to say it of Ally McCoist. He has a massive fan following and is in constant demand for appearances, endorsements and a wide range of other activities. He revels in it but it has never changed him. His feet are firmly on the ground, he dotes on his family and he is still the same nice guy that started his professional career with St Johnstone in 1979.

Let's hope that he does continue at the top well into the next century. There will never be another Super Ally.

Willie the Warrior

I COULD not put together a book like this without paying tribute to one of Scotland's greatest servants and a player whom I admired throughout his career — Willie Miller, a true warrior of the Highlands.

Willie had the heart of a lion. He led by example, never shirked a tackle and was a tremendous captain for both his club and his country. He was never one of those players who was going to be in constant demand for personal appearances and television advertising but, believe me, Willie was everything that a professional footballer ought to be.

Miller began life on 2 May 1955, in Glasgow. Like the rest of us Glaswegians he was football daft and always wanted to be a professional. All Glasgow lads wanted to either play football or be train drivers in those days. Nobody wanted to be a doctor or a miner or something like that. Willie was no exception.

He played for his school soccer team and was then in action for a side called Eastercraigs. A scout for Aberdeen recommended him and, not long after his 16th birthday, he was on his way to Pittodrie as a new youth player. It was not only the Dons who were impressed. He soon made his debut in the Scotland youth international side and his performances confirmed that Aberdeen had made a good move in signing him. Little did they realise just how good a move it was.

After two seasons of youth and reserve-team soccer, Willie was finally given his chance in the first team. His League debut was away to Motherwell on 1 September 1973 in a League match in the old Scottish First Division. It was a hard-fought goalless draw, but Willie came off the pitch with as big a grin as if the Dons had just secured a major victory.

It was the start of something big for both Willie and Aberdeen. By the end of the season he had made 31 League appearances for the Dons and had even managed to get his name on the score-sheet for the first time. His international career progressed as well as he steadily developed from a youth team player to the Scotland under-21 and under-23 sides. It was only a matter of time before he would be awarded his first senior cap.

Before that, however, there were many things to achieve with Aberdeen. The club had been buzzing around the top of the league for many years and occasionally had a bit of silverware as something to show for their efforts. They were about to enter one of their most successful periods when Alex Ferguson became manager in 1978. With Fergie in charge and Willie Miller as warrior-in-chief, the Dons went on the rampage.

In 1980, Aberdeen won their first League championship for a quarter of a century — and then repeated the feat in 1984 and 1985. The Scottish Cup was won three times in succession, in 1982, 1983 and 1984, and then again in 1986 when the Scottish League Cup was also captured.

Willie's finest hour was probably in 1983 when Aberdeen won the European Cup-winners' Cup — beating Real Madrid 2-1 in Gothenburg. It was certainly a night to remember for Willie.

"It was a fantastic achievement for us. We were confident that we could do it but nobody else really took us seriously. You couldn't blame them. You would not expect a giant club like Real Madrid to be beaten by a team from Scotland. A late winner killed them off though and there were celebrations for months afterwards."

Alex Ferguson left for Manchester United in 1986, but the Dons continued to be one of the dominant factors in Scottish football. They did not win the championship again but they did take both the Scottish Cup and the Scottish League Cup in 1989-90, thereby taking Willie's personal medal haul to ten.

One of his team-mates during those heady days of the early 1980s was Gordon Strachan, who firmly believes that Willie Miller was one of the chief reasons for the team's success.

"Willie was a great player. He never stopped working and he was formidable in defence. There are some players who always make you feel grateful that they are on your side and not among the opposition. Willie was just that sort of player. He gave everyone confidence and even when you felt ready to drop, the very fact that he was still going as strong as when the game first started, gave you renewed energy."

So you can see that I am not the only one who admired the tremendous talent of Willie Miller.

By the time he had completed his playing career, Willie had made an amazing 556 League appearances for the Dons — a club record that will take some beating. His very last League match for them was on 2 May 1990, in a 3-1 away win at Celtic. What a way to go! Aberdeen were runners-up in the Premier League, but had taken both of the major cups.

We have already touched on Willie Miller's international career — but touching is not nearly enough. He wore the shirt of Scotland with pride and honour. His senior debut for his country was on 1 June 1975 in a difficult match against Romania in Bucharest. I had played my last game for Scotland just four months earlier, but I was still taking as keen an interest as any other Scotsman who wants his country to be successful.

Willie had a very good debut and Scotland came away with a 1-1 draw, thanks to a Gordon McQueen goal. Just as you might have expected, Willie Miller played a passionate game — almost as if it was a World Cup Final and he had been in the side for years. What amazes me is that it was nearly three years before he was selected again.

His second cap came in February 1978 against Bulgaria in Glasgow. Willie put in his usual performance and Scotland won 2-1. Another 17 months elapsed before he was given a third chance, this time against Belgium in Brussels. Scotland lost 2-0 and, once again, Willie disappeared from the selectors' address book until the end of that 1979-80 season. Six months and four games after the Belgium match, Willie Miller was back in the side. The mission was to beat Wales in the Home International Championship. Probably he was only called up again because Graeme Souness had suffered a knock a few days earlier in a defeat by Northern Ireland. Willie rose to the occasion once again and scored the only goal of the game. Now he could not be ignored any more.

Before his international career ended, Miller collected 65 caps — the last against Norway at Hampden Park on 15 November 1989. Scotland needed not to lose in order to qualify for the 1990 World Cup. A goal from Ally McCoist was enough to earn the draw and 64,000 fans celebrated along with the players and officials.

Although Willie was not named in that World Cup squad, he had already played in the 1982 and 1986 tournaments and more than deserved his place in Scotland's Hall of Fame.

When Aberdeen hit a bad patch during the 1991-92 season, it was their former captain that they turned to. Alex Smith left the club in February 1992 and Willie Miller was immediately named as his replacement. The fans were happy and the future looked rosy.

Being a player is one thing, being a manager is something entirely different and, no matter how closely you worked with your own manager as a player and no matter how much you may learn from him, nothing ever prepares you for the day when you have to sit on the bench watching your players in action on the pitch. Willie Miller found it as frustrating as everyone else.

He had quite a good run at Aberdeen. When he took over as manager he was promoted from the coaching staff. The Dons were fifth in the table and they finished that season in sixth place. Willie loved the club and had great ambitions to push Aberdeen back to the top. He presented the board with a blueprint for success, which included major changes to the structure of the club to streamline its running and its finances. He proposed to put the emphasis on building up the youth squad and using it to service the first team. Players between the two, who did not make the first-team squad, would be moved on at the end of each season. There would be no selling of key players to keep the books balanced.

Willie felt that this would go a long way toward helping the club's shaky finances and, at the same time, build for the future with home-grown talent. He wanted to cast the net wider to find talent from further afield. It all made sense but, during the next couple of seasons, Aberdeen still failed to win a trophy and, unfortunately, patience is not something found in abundance at football clubs. Supporters have a few moans, phone local radio stations and write letters to the press, which then causes the board to get nervous and, in a bid to be seen trying to do something, the manager becomes the prime target.

I'm not suggesting that this is what happened at Pittodrie, but Aberdeen were League championship runners-up in both the 1992-93 and the 1993-94 seasons. They reached the Scottish Cup Final and the Scottish League Cup Final — but they did not actually win anything. The spirit drained very quickly and finally, in November 1995, the inevitable happened. Willie moved on and Roy Aitken became boss.

It was a blow for Willie Miller but one from which he quickly recovered and today he is as effervescent as ever — and still has Aberdeen etched on his heart.

He can look back on his career with satisfaction. He is still the last captain, other than an Old Firm skipper, to hold the Scottish championship aloft. That was back in 1984-85 when the Dons retained the trophy they had won the previous season. Yet Willie is not the sort of person to see that as a proud conclusion. He still cares passionately about his old club and would dearly like to see them take the title again.

"I doubt that we shall see another Aberdeen side like that of the 1980s," said Willie. "We had quality players, the right balance and the proper mental attitude all at the same time. Every now and then someone will mount a serious challenge to Rangers and Celtic, but it takes a really special set of circumstances for a provincial club to be successful. There is a big responsibility for Aberdeen to show the way.

"The Dons are the only club with the financial clout to get anywhere near Rangers and Celtic. It's vital for them to spend their money wisely and mount a serious challenge. And nobody will be cheering them on any louder than me."

That is typical of the spirit of Willie Miller. The burning desire to succeed still pulses through him just as it did when he was wearing the red shirt of Aberdeen. He was, indeed, a battler from start to finish …a great football warrior!

King Kenny

NOW we come to a real class act — King Kenny himself! A lot of people have completely the wrong impression about Kenny Dalglish. They believe him to be stand-offish, interested only in making money and playing golf. Nothing could be further from the truth. He is a shy sort of a guy who does not welcome media attention but does realise that it is a fact of life. Whatever he has made from the game he has earned — and it is the game itself which is most important to him. He is so wrapped up in soccer that he could appear on *Mastermind* and answer questions on the game and I'm sure that he would win. He is a soccer buff who can tell you exactly who plays where and what the result was in the Scottish Cup Final of 1958. Make no mistake — Kenny Dalglish IS football!

The Dalglish story began on 4 March 1951 when he was born in Glasgow. He was a big Rangers fan but was never destined to play for them. He became well-known in schools soccer and especially in local youth football. Playing for Glasgow United he was pitched against lads much bigger and older than himself, but he shirked nothing and even in those days could twist and turn himself around most defenders.

It was while he was playing for Glasgow United that he was seen by a Celtic scout. He wished it had been a Rangers scout but still accepted the invitation for a trial at Parkhead. He was successful of course and was offered a place in their junior side, Cumbernauld United. While he was with that junior side, the big boys of Celtic were winning the European Cup. In 1968 he became a full professional and part of that marvellous set-up of the Jock Stein era.

"I thought that it was just incredible to be playing in the reserves at that time," said Kenny. "I looked upon it then as the highlight of my career. When you think that we had players like Danny McGrain, David Hay, Vic Davidson, George Connelly and Lou Macari in our reserve side, it is not surprising that we did so well. We could probably have won one of the other divisions of the Scottish League if we had been given the chance. Almost as a body, we later moved into the first team and continued the Celtic success story."

I remember seeing Kenny when he was 17, and he was quite outstanding. It was obvious that, despite his youth and rawness, he was going to be very special. He had a very natural talent with good ball control, use of both feet, pace, ability to shield and to distribute, and also terrific aerial prowess.

When the great Bobby Murdoch was injured Kenny was given his first-team chance in October 1969. Celtic won the game 7-1, which was quite a debut to remember. He stayed in the side for a while but, when Murdoch recovered, he went back to the reserves for a while.

Initially, Celtic looked upon their 'find' as a midfielder — until they played him as centre-forward in a testimonial match. He scored six goals that night and every one of them was different — showing how much he had to offer in an attacking role. Celtic decided to develop that and gave him the chance to show what he could do as a striker in the reserves. Kenny delivered and Celtic suddenly found that they had on their hands a tremendously versatile young player with a deadly eye for scoring goals.

It was not long before he established himself permanently in the first team, and he eventually became captain of the side. His years in the team kept the Celtic trophy-collecting machine at full blast as the Bhoys swept to that magnificent nine League championships in a row from 1966 to 1974. He also collected five Scottish Cup winners' medals and the Scottish League Cup.

"I won League championship, Scottish Cup and League Cup medals during my time at Parkhead and I can honestly say that I enjoyed my time there. It was fantastic to travel away with such a huge and loyal set of supporters. People often ask me which of the cup finals or championships proved to be the highlight of my time with Celtic but, in fact, most of the memorable moments were those various changes and debuts in my progress."

There were even more changes to come. When Kevin Keegan left Liverpool in 1977, Bob Paisley knew that he would have to find someone a bit special to replace him. He did not look any further than Parkhead because he knew that he would find no-one better or more appropriate than Kenny Dalglish. Paisley created a new club transfer record when he splashed out £440,000 for Kenny — but it was to prove to be a tremendous investment. Can you imagine what Kenny would cost these days?

His last game for Celtic was in May 1977, away to Motherwell in a 2-2 draw, Kenny scoring the second of Celtic's goals. That was on the last day of the season. His Liverpool debut was on the first day of the following season in a 1-1 draw away to Middlesbrough. He scored the Reds' goal and sent the fans home happy. They became happier still during the following weeks as he scored in five of his first six games and helped Liverpool to remain undefeated for their first 13 League matches. By the end of the season, he had not only claimed 20 League goals as the club's top scorer, but he had also very quickly replaced Kevin Keegan in the hearts of the Liverpool fans.

It was the start of an exciting new chapter in the career of Kenny Dalglish. He had won a huge collection of medals with Celtic but there were still many more to come at Anfield. He had settled in very quickly and, after just one season, it seemed as if he had always played in a Liverpool shirt.

"There is no way I was scared of playing in England," Kenny recalled. "I missed home and friends for a while at first, but once my wife, Marina, and the two children we had then, Paul and Kelly, came down to join me in a new house, I felt very relaxed and happy."

He was especially happy at the end of that season. Liverpool did not win the Football League championship and neither did they win the FA nor the League Cup — but they did reach the European Cup Final where they had to beat FC Bruges of Belgium in order to retain the European crown which they had won the previous year. Although the game was to be played at Wembley, there were no doubts that it was not going to be easy for Liverpool. Indeed, they were fully stretched by the Belgians until Kenny popped up to score his 30th goal of the season and the one that really mattered in this European Cup Final.

"Sometimes words are just not enough to explain a feeling," said Kenny. "Winning that night was unforgettable. It was nearly too much to take in all at once."

A full house at Wembley that night would agree. Kenny had heard much of Celtic's 1967 European Cup triumph, but he had not actually been in the team. He had sometimes had the feeling that if only he had been born a couple of years earlier he might have had a European Cup medal in his possession. Now, that no longer mattered. He was one of the kings of Europe with his new club.

The medals came thick and fast again after that. He continued playing for Liverpool until it was time for him to hang up his boots. His final appearance was as a substitute for Jan Molby on 1 May 1990, in a 1-0 win over Derby at Anfield. It was a rousing finale since Liverpool were League champions and the fans had a chance to give him a final salute as a player.

By this time of course, Kenny Dalglish was no longer just a player. He had taken over as player-manager from Joe Fagan in May 1985, and a year after that was celebrating Liverpool's achievement of the League and Cup double. Once again he had added to his incredible toll of medals and personal honours and records.

In all, his Liverpool career had earned Kenny another eight championship medals, two FA Cup winners' medals, four League Cup winners' medals, three European Cup winners' medals and a European Super Cup winners' medal.

Add his Celtic medals to those he won with Liverpool and

Kenny has one of — if not THE — greatest collection of domestic honours ever assembled by one man. He also won countless personal honours, including Footballer of the Year in England in 1979 and 1983, PFA Player of the Year in 1983, and Manager of the Year in 1986, 1988 and 1990. There was another Manager of the Year award still to come in 1995 — but before then was the bombshell!

To say it was a shock would be an understatement. The Liverpool fans were completely stunned when the news broke on 22 February 1991 that Kenny Dalglish had resigned because of the pressure of management. They had assumed that he would remain a part of the Anfield furniture for the rest of his life and to many an outsider it had certainly seemed like that. Kenny needed a break, and that is exactly what he got with plenty of spare time to spend with his family and with his golf clubs.

However, he could not completely turn his back on football and, later that year in October, he was appointed as manager of Blackburn Rovers — who were ambitiously striving to get out of the Second Division. A win in the Wembley play-off at the end of that season, beating Leicester 1-0, was good enough to achieve that ambition, and Kenny was back in charge of a side in the top division.

The Blackburn story has been well chronicled since then. With Jack Walker's money they were transformed into a side more than capable of rubbing shoulders with the very best, and there was no better proof of this than when they won the Premiership championship in 1995 — interrupting Manchester United's flow of titles. As he steered the side to success, Kenny once again picked up a number of personal honours including that Manager of the Year award we mentioned a short time ago.

There was yet another shock to come, however, when Kenny once again decided to vacate the manager's chair, at first moving upstairs as director of football at Ewood Park and then finally quitting the club.

They say that you can't keep a good man down and I think that Kenny will continue to be in the game for some years to come now that he has returned with Newcastle.

I mentioned that I knew Kenny when he was just 17 but, of course, our paths have crossed many times since then. He made his international debut at Pittodrie when Belgium were the visitors in November 1971.

"Those are the type of dates that you do not forget," recalled Kenny. "Scotland beat Belgium 1-0 and I came on as substitute for Alex Cropley. I was thrilled to bits when I went out on to the pitch. I had badly wanted to play for my country and now it had finally happened.

"My first full game for Scotland came one month later — but we lost 2-1 in Holland. I found the change from League football to international football both interesting and challenging. I was very conscious of wanting to establish a good level of consistency and hold on to my place."

I remember Kenny's early games very well. I was playing in most of them and did so until just after our 1974 World Cup campaign. By the time I disappeared from the inter-national scene, Kenny had already won 25 caps and he was still only 23. From the moment he made his debut it was clear that he was going to be a part of the Scotland squad for some time to come. He never once looked out of his depth, even when we were playing in the World Cup among all those great players and in front of millions of television viewers.

Kenny's last game for Scotland was at Hampden on 12 November 1986, in a 3-0 win over Luxembourg. It was his 102nd senior cap. Long before that he had broken the Scottish record for caps and his final tally has put him into, what looks like, an unassailable position. At the same time he had scored 30 goals for his country, equalling Denis Law's record total and is still joint leading scorer in the history of Scotland internationals. Whether or not that record will remain, only time will tell. Perhaps Mr McCoist might have something to say about that.

Kenny has had a fantastic career both as a player and as a manager and I am sure that he is by no means finished yet. I hope not because he has one of the keenest soccer brains in the business. He has a great understanding of both individual skill and temperament and also of team tactics. He learned his trade well from his managers and team-mates of the past but, unlike so many others, he has put that acquired knowledge into practice.

Great though he has been as a manager, my favourite memories of Kenny are as a player. He had fantastic vision and could both score goals and create them for others. As good as Ian Rush has been, Kenny Dalglish provided him with the perfect foil when they were both in Liverpool shirts. Nothing was too difficult for Kenny and his supreme confidence was an inspiration for all those around him.

Over the years Kenny has received many accolades. All I can say is that every bit of applause he has received during his time in the game has been thoroughly deserved. He really is the King.

Wembley Wizards

EVERY Scotsman who has ever kicked a football has wanted to be in a side that beat England. There is just something about putting one over on the Auld Enemy that makes it a more important quest than any other. Beating foreign opposition is always a good reason to celebrate — but beating England is the signal for parties in the streets.

Probably the greatest international upset of all time in the clashes between Scotland and England came on 31 March 1928 — the day of the Wembley Wizards. Possibly an Englishman would never fully understand what all the fuss was about — but to Scotland it was far more than that convincing score-line. It was the manner in which a team of so-called Scottish no-hopers humbled mighty England on their own hallowed turf.

When the Scottish team was first announced for that game it was instantly written-off by many. There was criticism that it contained too many 'Anglos'– a name given to Scots who were playing their regular football in England. I have always hated that term. I have been called an 'Anglo' myself, but I can promise everyone that I am a Scot through and through and that I have played my heart out for Scotland just as much as anyone living north of the border. Being called an 'Anglo' makes you sound like some sort of second-class Scot and I deeply resent that.

In 1927, England had visited Hampden and won 2-1. Scotland wanted revenge — and to add a little more spice to the contest, as if it needed any, there was the added incentive that whichever side lost would be finishing bottom of the Home International Championship table. That's why interest in the game was at its peak when the side was announced. There were amazing scenes in those days, the like of which are never experienced today.

On 21 March 1928, a large crowd of several thousand supporters packed into Carleton Place, Glasgow, which was then the address of the Scottish Football Association. They were there to hear the official announcement of the team to face England. The traffic was halted and police marshalled the crowd as if they were actually at a match.

Nobody wanted to see Scotland finish at the bottom of the table, but they knew it was going to be a tough task playing away to England who would be putting out their big stars — Dixie Dean, Roy Goodall, Joe Bradford and goalkeeper Ted Hufton of West Ham — who was considered in those days to be the best in the world between the sticks.

That is why the crowd were rather tense as they waited for that Scottish FA official to stand at the top of the steps outside the Carleton Place headquarters and read out the names of the team who had the job of at least giving England a run for their money.

The first reaction was one of astonishment as the crowd learned that regulars Meiklejohn, McPhail and McGrory had been omitted from the line-up. The second reaction was one of annoyance when they discovered that only three players actually playing in Scotland had been named. There was disbelief that Bury's Tom Bradshaw had been picked to make his international debut — especially since he would have the unenviable task of marking Everton's prolific goalscorer, the great Dixie Dean. There was also some disquiet when the name of Hughie Gallacher was mentioned since he had been out with an injury for the past two months. Then there was another sharp intake of breath when it was realised that the forward line of Jackson, Dunn, Gallacher, James and Morton was the smallest attack team ever fielded by Scotland.

Newspaper reaction was much the same as that of the crowd. The headlines did not scream vitriolic abuse as they would have today, but comments like 'It's not a great side' — which was the offering of the *Daily Record* — were about as hysterical as you could get then. The general opinion among most Scots was that this was a side being taken like lambs to the slaughter. But the Scottish determination to cheer on even the most suicidal of lemmings prevailed and there could be no faulting of the spirit among the players or their followers.

England just about ruled football in those days and everyone considered that their failures against Wales and Ireland were little more than blips. Come the day of Scotland's visit and the stars of England would shine once again.

On the eve of the match, the Scotland players and officials were gathered in a London hotel, aware that everyone was talking about just how many England would score, rather than IF they would score. Somehow this only added to the team spirit in the Scotland camp and strengthened their will to win. After dinner, an official suggested to Scotland skipper, Jimmy McMullan, that he should give his players a pep talk in preparation for the game next day. He stood up and made one of the shortest tactics talks on record, saying, "Go to bed — and pray for rain!"

Amazingly, when they climbed out of their beds next morning, it was indeed raining. Over breakfast Jimmy looked at his small forward line — of whom the tallest was only 5ft 7ins — and said; "You've got nice weather for it lads!"

By the time they set off for Wembley, the rain had developed into a downpour and the advantage to the lighter Scots was growing. They would be able to twist and turn much more effectively than would England's heavyweights in those slippery conditions.

There is something very special about playing at Wembley, whether it is an international or a cup final, and that day was certainly no exception. The crowd of 80,868 had put on a brave face against the weather and for two hours before the kick-off there was an enthusiastic spell of community singing. Meanwhile, in the Scottish dressing-room, Jimmy McMullan was talking to 19-year-old defender Tony Law to calm his nerves, while Alex James was in a blind panic. He was not at all concerned about the game — but about his shorts! He had a reputation for wearing baggy shorts and he was not at all happy with the much briefer ones that he had been given. An official had to go out and buy another pair, returning just in time for Alex to maintain his 'baggy' image.

And so to the game. Despite the soaking and the community singing, the supporters were still in fine voice and gave both teams a rousing welcome as they took the pitch. Once the preliminaries were over the teams lined up and faced each other like David and Goliath. The referee blew his whistle and the Scots in the crowd had their hearts in their mouths almost immediately. The very first England attack resulted in Smith belting the ball past Harkness — but instead of it making a bulge in the back of the net, it smacked off the post and rebounded back into play. Jimmy McMullan fastened on to the loose ball and sent James and Dunn away. After an interchange, James slipped the ball to Alan Morton who took it almost into the corner before sending a perfect cross right into the area. Alec Jackson flew in from the other wing and headed the ball past the groping Hufton.

Scotland were a goal up inside three minutes and now the Scots in the Wembley crowd were rejoicing. England threw everything into getting an instant equaliser but Harkness, in the Scottish goal, had settled his nerves quickly after that initial near-miss, and he pulled off several magnificent saves. England were rattled and their finishing suffered as their confidence began to drain away.

The downpour continued and, had they been weather experts, the Scottish selectors might have been able to claim that they had picked a side especially for the conditions. As it was, that Scottish forward line did indeed give the big England defenders a hard time. It seemed on the cards that

Scotland might well score again as England began to flounder. Ted Hufton's great goalkeeping reputation was certainly well deserved as Scottish pressure increased and he had to pull off a string of excellent saves to keep them at bay.

With the referee looking at his watch for the half-time whistle, Alex James picked up a bad clearance from the England defence. He dribbled past Wilson, then Healless and finally Jones before reaching the edge of the penalty box — and from there he unleashed a cannonball of a shot, low into the corner of the net, that gave Hufton no chance. There was barely time to restart the game before half-time and the Scots trooped off with their heads held high, while England was obviously plunging into a trough of depression.

What followed in the second half was one of the most memorable 45 minutes in Scottish football history. Conditions did not improve and yet, somehow, the Scots raised their game still further and played the sort of football that you would normally expect to see played on a perfect pitch by a team such as the Brazilians. I know it might sound biased but, if you don't believe me, just take a look at the newspaper cuttings from the time.

That diminutive forward line teased and tormented the England defence — often leaving them on their backsides — as they danced around with the ball. The Scottish midfield took complete control of the centre of the park and England were reduced to rare attacking forays. Meanwhile, the Scottish forward line played virtually at will and it was only a matter of time before they found the net again.

Alex James sent a drive crashing against the crossbar and then brought a magnificent save from Hufton. But Scotland were not to be denied. In a copy of the first goal, Morton took the ball almost to the corner flag before sending over another precision cross which Jackson met with his head. Scotland were 3-0 ahead and by no means finished. They were enjoying themselves and were going to make the most out of their afternoon out.

Moments after that third goal, Hughie Gallacher decided to get his name on the scoresheet and sliced forward through the England defence only to be brought crashing to the ground by a heavy tackle. Alex James pounced on the loose ball and hammered it into the net.

If this Scotland display was being shown on television nowadays, the pundits would be purring. Moves were made which strung together seven or eight passes — even 11 passes on one occasion. The midfield and forwards were playing so well that the Scotland defenders had time to applaud. England were demoralised at 4-0 down in front of their own supporters but, to their credit, they did not give up trying.

With only five minutes to go it was Morton who again drew the England defenders out of position by taking the ball into the corner before unleashing another marvellous cross — and there was Jackson rushing in again to meet the ball. This time he went for a spectacular mid-air volley and the ball flew into the back of the net to give him an historic hat-trick.

England were humiliated. I'm sorry, but there is no other word for it. In the last minute, Bob Kelly scored a magnificent consolation goal for them, hitting a 40-yard free-kick past Harkness — but the celebrations were muted.

At the end of the game the rain-sodden crowd applauded the performance. The England supporters were swift and warm in their praise of the Scots and the Scottish fans were justifiably delighted. There were no pitch invasions — no aftermath of violence. The crowd went to see a football match and had been treated to a legendary performance which has since become a part of soccer folklore.

Back in Scotland the pubs did rather well and the newspapers were not slow in piling praise on to the heads of those little no-hopers. The *Glasgow Herald* was a typical example when they said: 'Want of height was looked upon as a handicap to the Scots' attack, but the Scottish forwards had ability and skill of such high degree as to make their physical shortcomings of little consequence.'

Scotland skipper, Jimmy McMullan, took time out from the after-match celebrations to comment on the way that he saw the game.

"I want to emphasise that all our forwards are inherently clever," he said. "But I wish to say that the English tactics were wrong. The Saxon wing-halves paid more attention to the wingers than the inside-forwards — therefore the latter were given a lot of space. It is a common thing in England to let wing-halves, and not full-backs, mark the wingers. It doesn't pay and I don't know why they pursue it."

It was a gentlemanly comment. He did not belittle the English effort, or try to elevate his own side to the abnormal, but merely made an observation which was probably just about right. By adopting those tactics, England placed themselves at the mercy of a much underrated Scotland attack. The rain made matters worse for England too — but you cannot entirely blame the weather for a 5-1 drubbing at home!

To prove the point, Scotland won again the following year when the two sides met at Hampden. The scoreline was a more sober 1-0, but the result was all that the Scots had hoped for.

The Wembley Wizards of 1928 caught the imagination of all soccer-loving Scots. They had created a culture shock! Nobody could beat England at Wembley — let alone a little Scottish side with a forward line that looked as if it should have Snow White as captain. As a boy, the Wembley Wizards were all I heard about. If you could not rattle-off the team, consisting of Harkness, Nelson, Law, Gibson, Bradshaw, McMullan, Jackson, Dunn, Gallacher, James and Morton, then you were considered a soccer non-starter.

When you realise that I was born in 1942 and these heroes were still being celebrated in my growing-up time, more than 20 years after the event, it says something for just how much of a milestone in soccer history that result became.

It was also an historic day in the story of Wembley Stadium. In a booklet published by the stadium owners in 1945, the story is told like this:

'English football fans shudder when the year 1928 is mentioned. The traditional enemy, Scotland, came to Wembley and gave the Sassenachs a first-class lesson in the art of playing football. So much so that, to this day, that Scottish team is still spoken of as 'The Wembley Wizards'.

'All Scotland seemed to come to town for that match, and the fans actually brought their own scaling ladders to make sure of getting into the stadium. As a result of this, Wembley afterwards became a barbed-wire fortress.

'The King and Queen of Afghanistan were among the

mammoth crowd who saw the Scots make rings around England. It was Scotland's day without a doubt. Alan Morton, Glasgow Rangers' Wee Blue Devil, and Alec Jackson, then with Huddersfield and later with Chelsea, were on the Scottish wings and the English defenders just couldn't do anything about them. Also, of course, there was the great Alex James — he of the long pants who rarely scored a goal but made openings for hundreds.

'That great Scottish team is surely worth giving in detail. Here it is, with the clubs the players were associated with at the time: J. D. Harkness (Queen's Park), Nelson (Cardiff), Law (Chelsea), Gibson (Aston Villa), Bradshaw (Bury), McMullan (Manchester City), Jackson (Huddersfield), Dunn (Hibernian), Gallacher (Newcastle), James (Preston), and Morton (Rangers) …Ah! What a team!'

That was the verdict from the owners of the mighty stadium.

Celebrated soccer scribe, Ivan Sharpe, wrote: 'England were not merely beaten. They were bewildered — run to a standstill, made to appear utterly inferior by a team whose play was as cultured and beautiful as I ever expect to see.'

More than 30 years later he was still writing the same thing, adding that he had never seen a performance to match it in all the time that he had been watching football.

Those 11 Scots were heroes beyond compare. The title 'Wembley Wizards' says it all really, but perhaps the final word should come from one of the stars of that great day — Alex James.

When asked for his comment after the game, Alex simply beamed a smile and said, "We could have had ten!"

The Lisbon Lions

I WAS watching on television when the heroes of Celtic achieved what no other British club had done before. It was, of course, 1967 — and one of the greatest nights in the history of Scottish football. Celtic won the European Cup and the Lisbon Lions became a legend.

It had been a great source of frustration for some years that, season after season, we had been forced to watch as bystanders while Spanish, Italian and Portuguese clubs had played out the European Cup Final. No British club had even reached the Final, let alone won it, and that made it all the more sensational when Celtic put the record straight and brought the trophy home to these shores as conquerors of Europe.

Celtic were in the competition after winning their first Scottish championship for 12 years. They were to go on to win that title for a further, amazing, nine consecutive seasons, but even that record pales alongside the achievement of winning the European Cup. They did not just strike a blow for Scotland and Britain but for football itself as the competition had become increasingly dominated by, what was an Italian disease of the time, negative soccer. Soccer with so much emphasis put on defence that goals had become something of a by-product rather than the chief aim of the game.

Behind the success of Celtic was a man who became a legend in his own right — Jock Stein. More of Jock later, but in the year in which he had taken over as boss of Celtic he had revolutionised their game. First came the League championship and then came the tilt at Europe.

Celtic, in that very short period of time, had become what was probably the best club side that Scotland has ever seen. We have already mentioned Jimmy Johnstone and Billy McNeill, but when you look at the rest of that exciting side, you are looking at men who deserve a Hall of Fame all to themselves.

Wee Jimmy was totally unpredictable and destroyed the confidence of opposing defenders, Bertie Auld was a brilliant architect and had a great ability to read the game and to distribute the ball to exactly the right department. Bobby Murdoch had great ball control, a lovely passing touch, and power that was quite fearsome — especially if you were a goalkeeper trying to get in the way of one of his hot shots.

Tommy Gemmell was another of soccer's characters with great flair both as a full-back and a winger. Ronnie Simpson had such safe hands in the Celtic goal that virtually half the games he played for them ended with a clean sheet. Bobby Murdoch, Jim Craig, Bobby Lennox, Steve Chalmers, Willie Wallace and John Clark are all names that have become as much a part of Scottish lore as any other home-grown hero. If you like, they are all Rob Roys of the Rovers!

Celtic's progress in the European Cup had begun at Celtic Park in September 1966, when Zurich were the visitors for the first leg of the first round. It was a tough game with the Swiss side in determined mood. Tommy Gemmell opened the scoring and Joe McBride, top scorer the previous season, added another to give Celtic a useful 2-0 advantage for the second leg.

It was expected that the Swiss would throw everything at their Scottish visitors when the two sides met for the return leg of the tie, but it seemed that the defeat in Glasgow had taken the sting out of their spirit and, apart from some token threats, they capitulated. Celtic won 3-0 with Tommy Gemmell scoring twice, including a penalty, and Steve Chalmers adding another. To have won their very first European Cup tie by an aggregate of 5-0, against a team with a good reputation, was no mean feat. It gave an early indication that Jock Stein's refusal to try and play the continentals at their own game was the best possible decision.

The reward for their first round success was another difficult tie in the next round. Celtic were drawn against Nantes, the French champions, with the first leg to be played away. The game took place on 30 November 1966, and Celtic once again opted to play it their own way. Not for them the tactic of playing for a draw with the idea of taking the initiative in the home return leg. They sought goals from the start and McBride, Lennox and Chalmers each found the back of the net. The French wondered what had hit them. They managed to score one of their own but were definitely a demoralised side by the time they had trooped off their own pitch on the wrong end of a 3-1 scoreline.

A week later the two sides met again in Glasgow. The Frenchmen scored, but Johnstone, Lennox and Chalmers made it 3-1 again and Nantes returned home with a 6-2 aggregate ringing in their ears. It was with a note of mystery that Celtic greeted the draw for the third round of the competition. They were to play Vojvodina of Yugoslavia — which caused most Celtic fans to look at each other and asked, "Who?"

They soon found out who when, on 1 March 1967, they lined up to meet the Yugoslavian champions. Celtic found them to be a tougher nut to crack. They did not play in the same style as the other continentals. Their defence was more rugged and not so easily conned out of position. They relied on a sparse attack, but were also capable of swarming in numbers to multiply the threat, rather than leave it to a lone ranger. Celtic found themselves having to work unusually hard in protecting their own goal, and it took just one mistake for Vojvodina to score. The home side then threw up a wall to protect their lead and Celtic were forced to return to Scotland having suffered their first European Cup defeat.

The scene was set for yet another passionate night at Parkhead when the two teams met again for the return leg. The Yugoslavs were determined that their single goal was going to be good enough to get them through. Steve Chalmers had other ideas, and kept working until the visitors made a rare mistake. He needed no second chance and soon put the ball in the back of the net. At 1-1 it was anybody's game, and that is how it remained with almost a tug-of-war going on as both sides tried to steal a winner without losing the ground that they had already gained.

The minutes were ticking away and the referee had already looked at his watch when, at a crucial moment, one head rose above all the others. It was the skipper, Billy McNeill, in true never-say-die style. The ball cannoned from his head and Glasgow erupted. It was 2-0 on the night, and 2-1 on aggregate. Celtic were in the semi-finals, the sixth British club to get there. But could they go boldly on where none had travelled before them?

In trying to keep the momentum going in Europe while also defending their title at home and competing in major cup competitions, all clubs face the spectre of a massive injury toll. Celtic did not fare too badly but they had lost their goal ace, Joe McBride, before Christmas and now had to manage without him. He was to play no further part in the European Cup and so that win over Vojvodina had seemed to the club to be played with one hand tied behind their backs. When the next draw was made and Celtic were to play the highly regarded Czech side, Dukla Prague, Jock Stein knew that he was going to have to put a lot of responsibility on the shoulders of Willie Wallace, whom he had signed from Hearts in mid-season.

The first leg of the tie gave Celtic home advantage and the place was sold out once again. Jimmy Johnstone struck the first blow and Willie Wallace followed that with two great goals. Dukla Prague managed to score one themselves and, while everyone thought that the 3-1 scoreline was a great result for Celtic, there was an underlying concern that Dukla's goal could prove to be significant in the final analysis. That worry proved to be unfounded. The Czechs adopted the strangest stance for the return match a week later. Instead of going on the rampage to try to crack their Scottish visitors, Dukla Prague actually played a defensive game which both puzzled and delighted the Scots. The final score was 0-0 and Celtic had reached the European Cup Final by virtue of a 3-1 aggregate.

The Final was scheduled for 25 May 1967, in Lisbon. Celtic were to face the mighty Inter-Milan who had already won the crown twice in 1964 and 1965. Before that Celtic had some domestic issues to be resolved — and they resolved them in style. Before going to Lisbon for the showdown with the Italians, they had made a clean sweep of the Scottish League championship, Scottish Cup and Scottish League Cup.

Jock took his men to the Ayrshire coast to prepare for the big match. I can recall him writing a piece in the Celtic magazine in which he said: "It is important for Celtic's players to think they can win every match they play. But it is equally important for them to keep in mind that there is always the possibility of losing. If it should happen to be that we lose to Inter-Milan, we want to be remembered for the football we have played."

That was typical of the man. He sought victory but, if it was not to be, he still wanted a triumphant defeat.

While he was preparing his players at their training camp, he showed them a film of the 1960 European Cup Final between Real Madrid and Eintracht Frankfurt — the famous 7-3 thriller that the Spaniards had won at Hampden. Jock wanted his players to see the sort of standard that he was expecting from them.

"The formation of the side is not as important as the attitude," said Jock. "Attack should be in the mind." It certainly was.

Come the hour, come the man and, to a man, Celtic were ready for their massive test. Inter-Milan were favourites as might have been expected, but the Scots were unconcerned about reputations. They had a job to do and they had travelled a long way to do it. There was no way that they were going to be easy prey for the Italians!

Inter began in style, going immediately on to the attack in an attempt to paralyse their opponents before they had time to settle. The great Mazzola was their prime attacker and he was determined to make his presence felt. He was the club's chief hope because of the absence of another superstar, Suarez, who had been injured. Mazzola launched into his task with great gusto and Celtic knew that they had a game on their hands.

In the seventh minute it was Mazzola who began a move that could have killed the game there and then. Some interchange between the Italians led to Cappellini finding himself with only one defender and the goalkeeper to beat. He hesitated long enough for Jim Craig to get in a tackle. Some say it was fair, others say it was over-heavy. The German referee sided with the latter view, blew his whistle and immediately pointed to the penalty spot. Mazzola took the kick and sent Simpson the wrong way. The Italians were in the lead. Their fans celebrated and relaxed.

A lesser side might well have fallen apart at this stage — as indeed many have — but Jock's men stuck to their task. Inter were content to shut up shop. With only seven minutes gone, the game was won as far as they were concerned and they were happy to call early closing. By doing this, the Italians actually played into Celtic's hands. Inter were used to playing against similarly defence-minded sides — teams who would struggle to put together any sort of concerted attack in order to break down a regimented defence. Celtic was not a team like that!

By shutting up shop, Inter gave Celtic the initiative. The Scots could concentrate on attack and withstand the occasional burst from the Inter forwards. Tommy Gemmell was given the freedom to exploit the flanks and Celtic put up wave after wave of attack. To their credit Inter stood firm, although goalkeeper, Sarti, was probably the busiest man on the park. Sarti played like a man inspired, helped a little by the woodwork, as both Bertie Auld and Gemmell fired shots that ricocheted off the post and crossbar.

The battle raged as Billy McNeill urged his men on to even greater effort, and still the Italians held their ground. It was like watching a boxing match in which one of the contestants gets hit from pillar to post but does not actually hit the canvas. At one stage it seemed that Wallace must score when he suddenly fell to the ground as if his legs had been caught in a man-trap. They had ...Sarti had grabbed both his ankles to prevent him from kicking the ball. In the melee the referee had missed the incident and, when Celtic went in for half-time they were still bemoaning the decision — or the lack of it.

Jock was not interested in what might have been. He rallied his troops for the second half and sent them back out with Billy McNeill's encouragement ringing in their ears. The game restarted with the Inter goal under pressure. Things carried on much the same way they had in the first half. The Scots were tireless in their bombardment and might well have blown themselves out if they had not been so determined.

When Jock had talked to them at half-time he had told his players to be a little less predictable. The Italians were getting used to traditional crosses, so he told them to give them something else to think about — some low, hard crosses instead of the usual aerial attacks. Jim Craig remembered that at just the right time. Yet another long Inter clearance was swept out to him on the right. The Italians prepared for another high cross but, just as he was about to make contact with the ball, Craig took Stein's advice and sent it low to the other edge of the box where Tommy Gemmell was rushing in. Tommy's boot met the ball and the goalkeeper was a stranded spectator as Tommy sent that ball flying into the back of the net. It was the 62nd minute and the moment that Scotland had been waiting for.

I leaped out of my seat along with everyone else who was watching, either at that stadium in Lisbon or at home on the television. It was a great goal and thoroughly deserved. At last, Inter-Milan had hit the canvas.

Of course, it was just the equaliser. The match was not yet won but everyone, including the Italians, knew that Celtic had struck what would prove to be a mortal blow. The favourites had fallen. The underdogs were still on their toes and dancing, waiting for the chance to land another, and the winning, punch.

The coup de grace came with just six minutes to go. Inter

had tried to regroup their attack but without incident, apart from Ronnie Simpson getting a hefty kick on the shins well after he had gathered the ball. Celtic kept their cool. They were not going to fall for any spoiling tactics. Bobby Murdoch took the ball along the left touchline and decided to have a shot. He sent the ball hard and low towards the goal. Sarti prepared to gather it but, suddenly, Steve Chalmers appeared from nowhere and stabbed the ball into the net. The Italians' heads fell, never to recover.

The last stages of the game were more like party prep-aration time. The Celtic players kept calm and did not allow their excitement to destroy their concentration. The Celtic fans at the game were in good voice and already preparing to greet their heroes on the pitch. Back home the corks were already popping.

At long last the referee blew that final whistle and the party began. The scenes of celebration were so incredible that it took a full half-hour before Billy McNeill and his men could disentangle themselves from the ecstatic fans and clear a path to climb the stairway and receive the magnificent trophy.

Bill Shankly was so excited that he rushed over to Jock Stein and gave him a big hug, before telling him — "Jock — you're immortal!"

Even Helenio Herrera, manager of Inter-Milan, paid tribute when he said, "Celtic deserved to win. We lost, but the match was a victory for sport."

At last a British team had won the European Cup, and fans all over England joined the Scots in their celebrations. It was not just that Celtic had won, not just that a Scottish team had won, nor even that a British team had won. It was the style in which Celtic had triumphed that earned the most applause. They were exciting, positive, determined and eager to play real football, no matter what the result.

To the names of the players and the manager add the name of Bob Kelly, the chairman who had given Jock Stein the job as Celtic manager in the first place and who had backed him all the way to this tremendous success.

Mainly, however, it was those 11 players who had done the work on the night. As they were walking through the tunnel to get on to the pitch at the start of the game, Jock Stein was leading them. He burst into song — 'Sure, it's a Grand Old Team to Play For ...'. Bertie Auld joined in and, before many more paces had been taken, the entire team were singing at the tops of their voices. The Italians were walking alongside them with all this ringing in their ears. It was their first encounter with this kind of passion.

Celtic kept up that song with their feet, playing their hearts out for the entire game. Simpson, Craig, Gemmell, Murdoch, McNeill, Clark, Johnstone, Wallace, Chalmers, Auld and Lennox — the Lisbon Lions and Scottish soccer heroes for ever.

The Class of '67

ACOUPLE of chapters ago I mentioned that there was nothing so satisfying to a Scotsman than to be in a team which beats England. I have to say that one of my most memorable matches was played at Wembley in 1967. It was not just memorable for me, but has gone down in soccer history as one of those games that stand out as a real national triumph. It stands alongside the great victory of the Wembley Wizards of 1928 as one of Scotland's finest hours, and I am proud to have been a part of it.

Remember, how could we ever forget, that England had won the World Cup in 1966. To his credit, Alf Ramsey had got the best out of his side and a strict 4-3-3 system. It hurt us Scots that England had won the World Cup. I wasn't that bothered myself but there were some, like Denis Law, who really hated the fact. He couldn't stand to hear about it, which is why he went to play golf rather than come into contact with the World Cup Final.

"The English had been on a high like never before," Denis later explained when talking about 1967. "They'd won the World Cup and their players and supporters figured that there was no-one in the world to touch them. As a young Scot, living and playing in England, it was a nightmare. You can't believe how much I wanted to beat them. I was desperate to bring them down a peg, and every Scot felt the same way. I always wanted to beat them but, in 1967, the emotions I felt were greater than at any other time in my career."

I think that the Lawman just about summed it up for all of us. We knew we had a good side and we were very disappointed that we had not qualified for the 1966 World Cup tournament ourselves. We considered that we had been unlucky and we knew that we were capable of beating England if we had the chance.

That chance eventually came on 15 April 1967. England had been unbeaten since a 3-2 defeat by Austria in October 1965. In fact that had been their only defeat in nearly three years. Everything was set up for our visit to Wembley with England being hot favourites to succeed — especially since we had a new manager. It was quite a baptism for Bobby Brown, but he set about the task in exactly the right way and had us all fired up from the moment that we gathered together to prepare for the game.

I think that, if anything, the English attitude was one of complacency. One London newspaper wrote: "I do not see it as being a repeat of the 1961 9-3 scoreline. I cannot see the Scots scoring three goals."

As the game approached we noted that Jimmy Greaves had been selected in preference to Roger Hunt and we took that as a compliment. England were strengthening their world championship side to face the mighty Scots. Our preparations were excellent but we did not need a lot of motivating because we all felt the way that Denis had expressed. On the way to Wembley we were all totally committed to our task. Nothing short of victory would do.

In the dressing-room the mood remained the same. As we had travelled to the great stadium we had encountered thousands of Scots. It was almost as if we were playing at home. Later we found out that there were 30,000 of our countrymen in the stadium that day. They sounded more like 300,000, and the roar that greeted us when we emerged from the tunnel would have done justice to a home match at Hampden. It was fantastic.

There were some nerves in the dressing-room. It would have been a worry if there had not since that could have meant that we too had fallen victim to some form of complacency — and that would never do for us. Jimmy Baxter sticks out in my memory. He quietly talked about what he was going to do to humiliate this one or that one. We knew he meant it too!

Bobby Brown had sprung a few surprises, not the least being two new caps for such an important game. Ronnie Simpson was put in goal. It was a good move since Ronnie was to become one of those Lisbon Lions that we have been recently discussing. This, however, was Ronnie's debut ...and at the age of 36. The English press had a field day when they heard.

"My decision wasn't too difficult," Bobby Brown told reporters. "Ronnie is a reliable 'keeper, has years of experience, and is the ideal man in a crisis."

In contrast, the other new cap was Jim McCalliog, an adventurous midfielder who had been playing some great stuff for Sheffield Wednesday. Jim was only 20 but the manager had faith that he could do a job for us and nobody was about to argue with him.

The side had been chosen with the objective of controlling and dominating the midfield and to add numbers to the defence when necessary, but chiefly to provide a good foundation for the attack. It had been well thought out by the Scotland boss.

I remember walking out for the introductions before the game and being amazed by the fans. I couldn't, however, let that deflect me from how I felt about the coming game. All my concentration was motivated toward that 90 minutes ahead. The noise of the supporters made the hairs on the back of your neck stand up, and it made you feel really proud to be there in the centre of it all. Despite these wonderful feelings, we were all very much aware that there was a still a game to be won.

We all felt the same and it showed as soon as the referee blew his whistle to start the match. We launched into the game instantly. It seemed that we had waited a long time for this and at last were able to get on with it.

Jim Baxter wasted no time. As soon as he got the ball he began to perform in his own unique style, teasing the opposition. He had said that he was going to take the mickey out of the world champions and he did so right from the start. His amazing ball skills were never better as opponents lunged at thin air where a split second earlier the ball had been. Slim Jim was enjoying his day out at Wembley.

He was quite happy to stand on the ball and wait for us all to get into position or make the runs he required from us. If an Englishman challenged he would be sidestepped contemptuously or beaten by a well-aimed pass from the best left foot in British football at that time. He was like a matador with that same grace and arrogance, almost to the point of being provocative.

There was little more than ten minutes gone when both Bobby Lennox and Jack Charlton went down injured on our left wing. Both players looked to be in trouble but, after treatment, Lennox was able to carry on while Big Jack went off for about a quarter of an hour. When he returned he went into a centre-forward position rather than take up his place in the heart of the defence.

Later, some English reporters pointed out that the injury to Big Jack and the knocks and strains to Greaves and Ray Wilson had ruined their game plan, and that the Scotland victory was little more than a large slice of luck. Don't you believe it — we played 'em off the park. Bobby Lennox nursed his injury throughout the game and Denis picked up an ankle injury before half-time, but ignored it for the rest of the match.

Scotland took the initiative from the start. We were not going to pay England the sort of respect that means you allow them to dominate the tactics and pace of the game. We were there to hustle, and that rocked them back because, usually, it was England's style to hustle the opposition. Geoff Hurst and Jimmy Greaves were meant to be England's goal-threat to us, with Alan Ball fetching and carrying and Bobby Charlton doing a bit of both. As we took a stranglehold on the game, however, the English midfield was pinned back and Hurst and Greaves were left stranded.

Bobby Moore was as outstanding in the English side as always, but even he found the Scottish pressure too much to handle. Ironically, we were down to ten men for a while after England had lost Jack Charlton. Tommy Gemmell had to receive treatment after a tackle by Wilson and he was stretched out behind the England goal when Wembley suddenly exploded. A free-kick came across the pitch to Willie Wallace. He tried a quick shot but it was blocked. The ball fell to Denis who needed no further invitation to go for goal. Gordon Banks pulled off a great save but could not hold on to the ball and the lightning reaction of the Lawman put it into the net. We were a goal up and the Tartan Army erupted like a volcano.

We knew that we had England by the throat now and we settled down to dominate even more. There are those who said that we could, and should, have scored several more in that first half, but perhaps they did not fully understand that we had come to do more than just beat England. We wanted to put on a show!

Nobody wanted that more than Jim Baxter of course. Before the game, when we were in the dressing-room, he was laying bets with me as to how many times he would 'nutmeg' various players and he was determined to win his bet. He totally tormented the England defenders and, for a while, even I started to feel sorry for them — but not for long!

When the first half came to a close we were a goal to the good and on top of the world. The England supporters had been silenced and our own were singing their heads off — everything was going according to plan.

England came out fighting in the second half. Their pride

was wounded and they wanted to repair the damage — but we were having none of it. We wanted to score more goals, of course, but we were still keen to demonstrate our supremacy over the world champions by a display of pure Scottish football.

We countered England's fight and a shot whistled past Gordon Banks' post after I took the ball away from Martin Peters. England took heart from being only one goal in arrears and Alan Ball set off on a great run on the left wing. His pass found Bobby Charlton who fired in a typically fierce shot which was blocked. The ball went into the air and it was Bobby who met it first, heading goalwards. Ronnie Simpson saw it late but still managed to drop on it, right on the goal-line. There were a lot of English protests that the ball had crossed the line — but I was there and I know that it hadn't.

It signalled a bombardment from the English. Bobby Charlton headed just over the bar, John Greig headed another off the line, and then Ronnie Simpson made another great save when he dived at the feet of Geoff Hurst. You could sense the frustration in the English camp and among their fans as they threw everything at us for a few minutes but still had nothing to show for it.

We hit back and England were forced to defend, which frustrated them even more. Jim Baxter was having the time of his life.

"I enjoyed taking the mickey out of England any day of the week, but that day was special," said Jim. "Alan Ball's voice kept rising another couple of octaves to the point that no-one could even make out what he was trying to say. Tommy Gemmell had passed the ball about and had Balley dashing backwards and forwards in an attempt to break up our game, and making him angrier and angrier with every pass. It was wonderful. How many guys can say that they played 'keepie-up' in the middle of Wembley during an England-Scotland match?"

With a quarter-of-an-hour left we pushed even harder for another goal and there was just 12 minutes on the clock when England cracked again and Bobby Lennox drove home after bursting through their defence. It was 2-0 to Scotland and the Tartan Army were going crazy. Yet the game was far from over. It had been an exciting match which I felt that we had controlled totally — but the last minutes turned it into a real thriller.

England were desperate to salvage something from the situation and threw all caution to the wind in an all-out attempt to grab a goal. With just five minutes to go Jimmy Greaves suddenly popped up and back-heeled to the onrushing Ball. He sent a low centre into the box and it was Big Jack of all people, playing at centre-forward, who got on the end of it and sent the ball into the net with the help of a deflection by the post.

It was a neat bit of football, even if the finishing was much more like that of a defender than a forward. Not to be outdone we sought an immediate reply and who else should step up yet another gear but the Lawman himself. Gordon Banks always named Denis first on his short-list of stars he most hated playing against. If you get the chance to see a replay of our third goal in that 1967 international you will understand why.

Denis did not score the goal himself, but he broke loose and sent a chip over Gordon Banks that had 'world class goal' written all over it. It needed a world class save to prevent it from going in, and Banks did just that. Somehow he got his fingers to the ball and stopped it from crossing the line. Wallace and McCalliog did not give him much time to settle down again, however, and a bit of quick footwork between the two ended with the net bulging. Gordon must have felt that he might as well have not bothered about saving from Denis.

The scoring was not quite over even now because, at the last minute, Geoff Hurst pulled another one back. There was barely a murmur from the England fans — they were too much in a state of shock to respond.

When the final whistle blew the scoreboard said — England 2, Scotland 3, but everyone knew that the result was much more profound than that. As Bobby Brown said afterwards: "We should have won by something like 5-2. Gordon Banks kept the score down."

The scoreline didn't seem to matter. It was the manner of the victory. The Wembley pitch was completely covered by ecstatic Scotland fans. Grown men were dancing like kids — I know because I was among them. London definitely belonged to the Scots that night as Trafalgar Square and all the other great landmarks of the city were visited by members of the Tartan Army who felt as if they had just conquered the whole lot.

Back in the dressing-room we were in celebratory mood too. Jim Baxter was trying to work out just how much he was owed from the various bets that he had made about making the England stars look foolish. Denis Law had a huge grin on his face and was shouting a lot. Ronnie Simpson was reflecting on what he thought was going to be the highlight of his entire career.

A month later, of course, he had changed his mind when Celtic won the European Cup.

As for me, I was thrilled to bits and kept reliving moments from the game. I could not stop talking about it — but I couldn't wait to see my family either. We were going to have a celebration that night, that was for certain!

England were world champions. We were the very first team to beat them after they had won their crown, and therefore that made us ...! Well, whatever it made us, we were certainly feeling on top of the world. The newspapers went crazy and hailed ours as one of the great performances of the century.

Today, whenever any of us are appearing at a dinner or other special function, that game is one of the chief topics of conversation. Everyone wants to know all about that 1967 victory over England.

The names of Simpson, Gemmell, Greig, McKinnon, McCreadie, McCalliog, Baxter, Wallace, Law, Lennox and Yours Truly, went into the book of Scottish soccer history as The Class of '67.

Super Bosses

S COTLAND does not just produce great players and, in this Book of Heroes, it would be wrong if we did not turn our spotlight on four of the greatest football managers of all time. They have become legends with their clubs and with their country. I am talking, of course, about Jock Stein, Bill Shankly, Matt Busby, and a 'young man' who is still very much alive and going strong — Alex Ferguson.

Two of those four played for Scotland themselves before they ever dreamed of becoming managers. Another was capped at various levels but did not actually make it into the senior side, although he later had the honour of being manager of his country at a World Cup. The fourth had no real international experience but still proved to be a great servant to his country.

I don't know what it is about us Scots. We have been hailed throughout the world as great doctors, great teachers, great scientists — all occupations which require a lot of patience. The same applies to being a successful manager. It can be the most frustrating job on earth. You have to be patient with your players, patient with your directors, patient with the supporters, patient with referees, patient with the press — in other words, you have to have more patience than your average family doctor

Knowing that most Scottish footballers are a pretty cavalier bunch, ready to take on the world at the drop of a bonnet, it is quite amazing that any of them ever do become managers. But we do — and we have a reputation for being pretty good at it. Let's take a look at four of the very best.

I knew Jock Stein very well and I was as stunned as everyone else when he died so suddenly after a Scotland game. It was not just that his death was such a great loss to football, but that it was such a loss to the world in general. He was a giant of a personality who had made an indelible mark. Soccer was enriched by his very presence and so were all those who knew him — in or out of the game.

Jock's beginnings were very simple. He was born in the same mining area of Ayrshire that yielded so many other soccer 'greats'. He went through the stages of schools and junior football and, basically, had the same choice as some of his equally fortunate contemporaries — a career in football or one down the mines. As a player, however, it hardly seemed as if he were going to have much of a career.

It is odd, really, that a man who later achieved so much should have had such a humble beginning to his soccer career. He began at Albion Rovers, then in the Scottish Second Division, and he stayed at the Coatbridge club for two seasons — from 1948 to 1950. In that time he played only 17 League matches and scored two goals. He was a half-back, keen in the tackle and accurate in the pass, but he did not exactly set the world on fire.

The strangest thing happened in 1950 when he moved

from Albion Rovers and joined Llanelli in the Welsh League. It was an unusual move, because most people would have gone to another Scottish club, moved to England, or just dropped out of the game. Jock, though, decided to be different and have a go at making a name for himself in Wales. He kept his house in Hamilton just in case anything went wrong and it was a good job that he did.

On the downside, Jock's house in Scotland was twice burgled while he was in Wales, and he didn't seem to be getting anywhere with Llanelli. Pretty fed up, he decided to call it a day and was actually on his way to see the manager to explain that he wanted to quit, when the Llanelli boss walked up to him and said that there had been a phone call for him from Celtic.

Stein was ready to give up on football and try his hand at something else but that phone call made all the difference. He phoned Parkhead and was virtually signed by Celtic there and then. By the time the 1951-52 season was under way he was a Celtic player. The club had wanted him to add some stability to the reserve side and use his experience to help the young players coming through. It was not exactly stardom but it was a job in football.

It's funny how things can work out. The season was still young when both of Celtic's first-choice centre-halves were injured, leaving no choice but to put Jock into the first team. He was an instant success, obviously one of those players who improve in better surroundings. It was a revelation to the Celtic management who thought that they had just signed a make-weight who might do a job among the hopefuls.

In the 1952-53 season he proved his worth beyond all

question and was rarely out of the team, making such an impression that he became captain. The following season he led his men to a League and Cup double. Life had changed completely for him and he was at the top of his game until he sustained an ankle injury in 1955 which ultimately put an end to his playing career. He struggled on for a while, but it was obvious that he was never going to be the same player — especially since the injury had left him with a permanent limp. He retired from playing but Celtic kept him on as a coach, helping to produce such players as Paddy Crerand and Billy McNeill.

Jock remained with Celtic until he gained his first managerial job in 1960 with Dunfermline Athletic. When they appointed him they were in a desperate relegation situation with just eight games left to play. His brief was to prepare them for a quick return the following season. Instead he inspired the side to win six successive games and avoid the drop.

The following season Dunfermline was buzzing. The crowds came flocking back, the ground underwent improvements and the team won the Scottish Cup — the first honour that they had ever secured. Within a season and a bit, Jock had transformed Dunfermline from a provincial club with more hope than expectation, to a club that was a force in Scottish football.

He remained in charge until 1964 when Hibernian were in trouble and kept casting longing looks at the success of Dunfermline. Hibs were a bigger outfit and represented a greater challenge and so Jock decided to give them a try. The scenario was very similar to that which had been evident when he took over at Dunfermline. Hibs, too, were threatened by relegation and were in a very depressed condition.

Stein's arrival was like the waving of a magic wand. Results improved and soon Hibs were back on course for honours. They won the Summer Cup of 1964 and, the following season, turned into favourites for the Scottish League championship. It was then that Celtic stepped into his life once again.

It was on a pleasant morning in the spring of 1965 that the Celtic chairman, Robert Kelly, introduced Jock to everyone at Parkhead and then left him to it with the immortal words, "It's all yours now!"

Jock took him at his word and quickly settled in. Oddly enough, he was only the club's fourth manager since it had been formed back in 1888. He took over a club that was tearing its hair out for success. The League championship had not been won for 11 years — the last time being in 1954, when Jock was captain. The Scottish Cup had not been seen for the same period and the Scottish League Cup had been missing for seven years. To make matters worse, the Auld Firm rivals, Rangers, had been parading a fair bit of silverware during that same period.

Within three months of his appointment, Jock had gone some way to putting all that right. He guided his new club to the Scottish Cup Final, where they faced one of his old clubs, Dunfermline. After an epic battle, Celtic won 3-2 and, at last, there was a reason to buy some silver cleaner. The following season he went even further and steered Celtic to the Scottish championship and League Cup. They also reached the Scottish Cup Final and the semi-finals of the European Cup-winners' Cup. Jock received a personal accolade when he was named British Manager of the Year, and handed a cheque for £1,000.

What was the secret of his instant success? It was definitely not the cheque-book because, in all that time, he had not bought a single player. Jock once tried to explain it himself.

"I work hard for my players. I do everything in my power to help them, even to keeping up with the game elsewhere. I work to make them successful and they know this. I think I have won their respect and this I rate as the most important consideration. Discipline with respect is by far the best way."

Indeed, there is no doubt that he was respected by everyone. He had a wonderful way of motivating you. You would play your heart out for him simply because he knew what he was talking about — you knew he knew what he was talking about and he was such a nice guy with it.

The European Cup triumph came in 1967, and with it an amazing clean sweep of honours at home — and so Celtic went on during his time with them as manager. After having resisted all temptations to join other clubs — Manchester United among them — he finally decided to take up another challenge and became manager of Leeds United in August 1978. It lasted just 45 days. He had not signed a contract with the club and there was an immediate problem because his family did not like the place. At the same time, Scotland were looking for a new national team boss — and Jock was the obvious choice.

Stein had been in charge of the Scotland team on a temporary basis in 1965, but this was a permanent position.

He took Scotland to the 1982 World Cup finals and had virtually qualified for the 1986 finals, when tragedy struck. As the final group qualifying game against Wales in Cardiff ended in a 1-1 draw, Jock collapsed and died following a heart attack. The soccer world was stunned. It was so much more than just a loss to the game, it was a personal loss to all who knew him.

Jock had gained many honours during his career, and was known throughout the game as a very sincere, humble man, devoted to his family. Although he enjoyed so much success, he always maintained that his greatest satisfaction came from helping young players establish their careers as professional footballers.

There is a nice little story about Jock and his drinking habits — he didn't have any. He just did not drink and that was that. Once, before a Cup Final, Bertie Auld tried to coax him into changing the habit of a lifetime. "If we win, you'll have to have a drink with us," said Bertie. Sure enough Celtic won, and Bertie reminded Jock of what had been said before the game.

"Now Bertie," said Jock. "Would you think any the more of me if I had a drink with you?"

There was no answer to that, of course, as no-one could possibly have had a higher regard for the man than they already had. They would have walked across the sea to America for him.

Paddy Crerand knew Jock better than most and he summed it up very simply.

"He knew more about football than anybody that I've ever met."

Paddy has met quite a few, I promise you ...but there, nobody has ever met anyone quite like Jock Stein.

Bill Shankly was a totally different kind of character, although there were quite a few similarities between the two. Stein stealthily gave players self-belief, while Shankly bristled, and roared that they were the best in the world and that all the rest were not fit to clean their boots. Both of them turned their backs on drinking, they would both die for their players, and both had a sense of humour and the keenest of soccer brains. They were also very good pals.

Shankly was born in a little mining village called Glenbuck. You can hardly see it now as it gently decays amid the Ayrshire countryside. In Shankly's youth, however, it was a busy little place. Just about every male worked in the mining industry and came home to their large families and football. The local soccer pitch was the focal point of village life, so it was no real wonder that Shankly and his brothers all became professional footballers.

Shanks started his pro career after his five older brothers had left home to pursue their own soccer adventures. He had already been working down the mines for a while but, when Carlisle offered him a chance at the age of 17, he did not hesitate. It was the start of a spectacular career that took him, after just a couple of seasons, to Preston, where he remained for the rest of his playing days — although he was a wartime guest for a number of other clubs.

He earned a massive reputation as a player for being one of the best half-backs in the game. He had tremendous leadership qualities and was totally dedicated to soccer. Not for him the beer and fags in the pub after a game. He had stringent beliefs about keeping in condition, and he admired people who took care of themselves.

Shanks was a tough tackler but could never be described as dirty. He lived by the sword and never cribbed when he was on the receiving end. He was a battler who never shirked his duty and always kept going from whistle to whistle. He never accepted defeat without fighting right to the end. Even if a cause was lost, he would still keep battling on until the referee called a halt.

It was that sort of determination that made him so outstanding as both player and manager. There's a nice little tale about Shanks listening to a speaker at a special dinner in his honour. The speaker said: "No finer wing-half than Bill ever pulled on a jersey." Bill leaned across to the person sitting next to him and said; "He's right you know!"

His great qualities as both a player and a person were major factors in Preston winning the FA Cup in 1938. The year before he had received a losers' medal when he was in the Preston side that lost 3-1 to Sunderland . The following year he was determined to make up for it, and Preston returned to Wembley and beat Huddersfield 1-0 to take the Cup.

Bill Shankly was immensely proud of being Scottish. He was thrilled to bits when he made his debut for his country against England in 1938, especially when Scotland won, 1-0. He hoped it would be the first of many such caps but, unfortunately, that was not to be as World War Two intervened. In all, Bill played five full internationals — four were victories and there was only one defeat, a 2-1 loss to England in Glasgow. Bill appeared in a number of wartime internationals and even managed to miss a penalty in front of the Kop while playing there for Preston. He admired the big clubs like Liverpool, but had no particular ambition to be in charge there one day.

Although he had stopped playing, Shankly was always more at home in kit than in a suit, and he was always very involved in practice matches and five-a-sides. He hated losing and sometimes the training matches would go on and on until his side was in the lead. He was also known to start out in the dug-out wearing a suit and then go to the dressing-room and change into full strip, boots and tracksuit, because it made him feel much more part of the game.

His legendary management career began at Carlisle immediately after he had retired from playing with Preston. From March 1949 to the end of the 1950-51 season he remained in charge at Carlisle. He did not win anything there but certainly vast improvement had been made, and Carlisle only just missed out on promotion from the Third Division North at the end of his last season with the club.

In July 1951 he moved to Grimsby, but he was not terribly happy there and his family were not very keen on living in the area. Grimsby had their moments during his reign, but no records were broken and no trophies were won. He felt frustrated by a club that, he felt, should be more adventurous and so, in January 1954, he resigned and took up another appointment as manager of Workington, who were then a League club, also in Division Three North.

Although he probably did not realise it at the time, Bill was really a big club manager. He soon became frustrated by a small-time approach. He was a polite man, but he didn't suffer fools gladly, and more than one club director felt the rough edge of his tongue during his management years. Workington fell into the small club category. Shankly thought that he could make sweeping changes, and in many ways he did, but they were not made quickly enough for him. The more he considered the matter, the more he realised that Workington were never going to be among soccer's elite. That was the chief reason why he resigned in November 1955.

Bill's old pal, Andy Beattie, offered him a job as coach at Huddersfield. Shanks willingly took on the job but it was not a good time for the two men. They had a number of differences of opinion. Later, they buried the hatchet and became good friends again, but those early days at Huddersfield were rather tense. Beattie became unwell later, in 1956, and the board decided to appoint Shankly as manager.

Huddersfield remained a Second Division club while he was manager, but he certainly made changes. He improved the club's youth policy tremendously with players like Denis Law, and England defender Ray Wilson beginning their careers under his guiding hand. In December 1959, Bill resigned after being offered a job that he just could not resist. He was approached in the club car park by a director of Liverpool and Shanks became instantly excited at the prospect of becoming manager of, what he considered to be, 'a sleeping giant'.

When the appointment became official it heralded the start of a new era for both Liverpool and Bill Shankly — and indeed for football in general. His influence on the game is still very evident today through people like Kevin Keegan, Terry McDermott, Roy Evans, Ray Clemence, Kenny Dalglish and many others. The book *The Shankly Legacy* reveals the debt that soccer still owes to the great man.

Liverpool were a Second Division side when Shanks took over. Within a few years, they were one of the greatest sides in Europe. Shankly brought his Liverpool backbone from Scotland when he signed Ian St John and Ron Yeats. Together, they took the club to incredible heights that saw major triumphs in the League championship, the FA Cup and the UEFA Cup. More than that, the foundation was put down for the great European nights to come.

In 1974, Shankly shocked Merseyside by announcing his retirement. He had little to do with Liverpool after that. He would turn up for an occasional game, but was just as likely to go and watch one of the other clubs in the neighbourhood. For a while he acted as a consultant at Tranmere and, most mornings, he would also drop in for a cup of tea and a chat with Howard Kendall at Everton.

He still loved to play the game and would enjoy even a kickabout with the neighbours and their kids. Sadly, in September 1981, he died and the world said farewell to one of the greatest characters that football has ever known.

Shankly was renowned for his wit, but I remember him at Wembley in 1965, when I was in the Leeds side playing against Liverpool in the FA Cup Final of that year. I was devastated at the end because we had lost quite a battle to his side. Shanks, of course, was delighted but, before his celebrations, he made a point of commiserating with us. Amid his personal joy he never forgot that human touch that made him so very special to all of us. He was a lovely man and a tremendous son of Scotland.

One of Shankly's big mates was also a major force in football, as well as being one of Shankly's own heroes — Matt

Busby. Just as Celtic still revere Jock Stein as a father figure, and Liverpool hail Bill Shankly as the man who made them what they are today, so Manchester United fans come close to removing their hats before they mention the name of Sir Matt Busby. He was another class act who made the sort of mark on the game that can never be overshadowed — even by the tremendous success of Manchester United in recent years.

Busby had a similar start in life to Shankly. He was born in the Lanarkshire mining village of Orbiston and had tragedy in his life when he was still a little boy. His father was killed in World War One and, at the age of six, Matt found himself to be the man of the house. His widowed mother also had three daughters, each of them younger than Matt.

By the time he was 15, Busby had followed his late father's former occupation and gone down the mines. Football showed him the way out, however, when he was playing for junior side Denny Hibernian and was spotted by a scout for Manchester City. He went to Maine Road in the late 1920s and made it into the first team during the 1929-30 season. There are probably few around now to remember it, but the half-back line of Busby, Cowan and Bray was said to be the best ever seen at Maine Road. It was this talented trio that steered Manchester City to the FA Cup in 1934. They had been at Wembley the previous season, but fell at the last hurdle when Everton proved to be too strong. They were determined to do better the following year and nobody was more determined than Busby.

The 1935-36 season was one of change for Matt. He was transferred from City to Liverpool and enjoyed the rest of his playing career at Anfield. He was playing up to the outbreak of World War Two, and had made such an impression at Anfield that they offered him a five-year contract as a coach, to commence after the end of the war. Busby did not take up the offer — although he might well have done if Manchester United had not come into the frame — and the knock-on effect could have been so very different.

Just imagine if the Busby Babes had been at Liverpool, and perhaps Shankly had become manager of United!

Matt was capped for the first time by Scotland on 4 October 1933, against Wales in Cardiff. The home side won 3-2, but Busby performed well and it was a foregone conclusion that he would be selected again. He wasn't! And it is still a mystery why the sum total of Matt's international appearances was just that one cap. During the war years he played for Scotland in a number of unofficial internationals and he also sampled the delights of management for the first time.

Having enlisted in the army, Matt became a company sergeant major Instructor, which gave him a great deal of man-management experience. He also took charge of the British Army soccer team while, at the same time, he was allowed to be a guest player for a number of League sides in the limited competitions that were organised during those years of strife.

For a short time Matt was stationed in Scotland and became 'manager' of Hibernian for that period in his life, recommending a number of players who later joined the club and gave them one of the best runs in their history.

It was February 1945 when Matt was officially appointed manager of Manchester United. It was quite a challenge. The club was not in good financial shape and Old Trafford was a mess after being bombed. For quite some time, matches had to be played at Maine Road, while Busby's office was in a corner of a coal depot and training was carried out on a piece of waste ground — later to become a car-park.

The first public statement made by Matt is worth recalling because it turned out to be quite prophetic.

"I am determined that United shall provide the United public with the best in the game. It is my intention to develop young players."

Within a very short space of time his style of management was beginning to work. In 1948 Manchester United won the FA Cup with, what has been described as, one of the best performances ever seen at Wembley. While that was going on, he gave the club strength in depth by introducing a revolutionary youth scheme that drew some of the best young players in Britain to Old Trafford.

While the young players were learning their trade, the experienced players were getting on with the job of re-establishing the club as a major force in the English game. They were championship runners-up for four seasons out of five, until finally taking the title in 1952 for the first time since before World War One.

Behind the scenes at Old Trafford, the development of the young players continued, and the scheme was beginning to bear fruit as the FA Youth Cup was won five times. Gradually those young players were drafted into the first team and, by the mid-1950s, the names of young stars like Byrne, Edwards, Taylor and Charlton were on everyone's lips. The League was won again in 1955-56, and again the following season — and that meant that United were in the European Cup for both of the following seasons.

The dreadful Munich air disaster is still vividly remembered and is not for us to dwell on here. It was a tragedy that is still upsetting to recall. Matt fought for his life and won, and thus began a new era in the histories of both the club and Matt Busby. He rebuilt the side with the famous Busby Babes and, in 1968, there was not a dry eye in the house when United finally won the European Cup and the world watched as Matt Busby ran on to the Wembley pitch to hug Bobby Charlton, who had lived through the Munich experience with him.

The miner's son from Orbiston was knighted later that summer and, in January 1969, he announced his retirement — moving 'upstairs' to the boardroom. He took over the reins again for a while when his successor, Wilf McGuinness, left the club. Matt was there on the night that United won the championship again in 1993 and then, in January 1994, he died.

Sir Matt Busby was a gentleman. I met him many times and always found him to be a really nice chap with an incredible football brain. Like Shankly, he left an amazing inheritance to his club. Both clubs are still enjoying the success originated by these two men and, in the case of Busby, he also played a major part in the achievements of the man who is in his seat at Old Trafford today — Alex Ferguson.

It would be appropriate for someone to wave a red book under Alex Ferguson's nose and utter those immortal words — "Alex Ferguson — This is Your Life!" Red has always been a good colour for him. The much-decorated red of Aberdeen, followed by the even more vibrant red of Manchester United.

But it was blue that was the colour to set the Fergie soccer story in motion.

Alex Ferguson was born in Glasgow on 31 December 1941. It was a great way to celebrate Hogmanay and he has been celebrating ever since. Having played for his school and just about any other side that would give him a game, it was almost beyond question that his career would somehow be involved with the game. His first club was not one of the big boys however — he joined Queen's Park.

He'll never forget his senior debut because it was for Queen's Park against Stranraer on 15 November 1958 — and he scored. Just before his 20th birthday, he went to St John-stone and stayed there for four years. Next came Dunfermline and 66 goals in 88 games. Rangers had been keeping an eye on him and finally paid £65,000 for him in July 1967, to add some fire-power to their side. The 1967-68 season saw Fergie finish as Rangers' top scorer but, come a change of manage-ment at Ibrox, and he was on the move again in November 1969, when Falkirk paid £20,000 for him.

Ferguson was signed as player-coach, and he spent four happy years at Falkirk before signing for Ayr United in the summer of 1973. He was still playing in those days but injur-ies brought that side of his career to a close in April 1974, and a few months later he became a full-time manager with East Stirling.

Very little happened at Firs Park except for a continual struggle near the foot of Division Two of the Scottish League. With less than a full season under his belt, Fergie left. St Mirren proved to be a different prospect. He took over as manager there in 1975 and remained until 1978, during which time he took them into the Scottish Premier and was feted by the fans. Strange though it may seem, the board did not share the enthusiasm of the supporters and, in 1978, Fergie left in less than harmonious circumstances — lodging a claim for unfair dismissal.

That cloud proved to have a silver lining, however, since the key to Pittodrie was waiting, and with it the chance to manage one of the biggest clubs in Scotland. His early days with the Dons were not spectacular, but he was busily planning for the future. His guile elevated Aberdeen to a lofty position in the Scottish soccer society, especially when they won the League championship for the first time in 25 years in 1980, and then repeated the feat in 1984 and 1985. There were Scottish Cup and League Cup victories as well, but the finest moment came in 1983 when Aberdeen reached European Cup-winners' Cup Final in Gothenburg. Real Madrid were the opponents, and naturally the favourites, but Fergie's men delivered and won the trophy, 2-1.

It was a tribute to his success that Fergie was made Scotland manager for a time in September 1985, after the tragic death of Jock Stein, and was in charge for the 1986 World Cup tournament. It was also a tribute to him that, when Manchester United sought a new manager in October 1986, Fergie was the man they went for. It was a good move.

It took a little while for Fergie to settle but, through the 1990s, the United success story has been phenomenal. Winners of the European Cup-winners' Cup, three times champions, twice double winners — and the story goes on.

Fergie has admitted that Sir Matt helped him a great deal when things were not going so well in those first few years at

Old Trafford. Alex had a bit of a reputation for being abrasive. The truth is that he thrives under pressure, but that he is more of the ranting, raving school rather than having the calm and gentle approach. When there were calls for his sacking from United, Sir Matt was there to encourage him.

"I used to speak to Sir Matt every day, and he encouraged me to calm down and stop being so fiery. He taught me to relax and take things in my stride much better. It was because of him that I started to take piano lessons and learned how to enjoy my spare time.

"Sir Matt was of great help to me, a wonderful man. I have always considered it to be a great honour even to be mentioned in the same company as him."

I never played against Alex Ferguson, but I saw him play a number of times. He played for Scotland at various levels, but never as a full international — which is a pity because I think he could have done a good job for his country. I believe that he carried an injury for quite some time, and that must have held him back. Whatever he did not achieve as a player he has certainly made up for as a manager. His achievements have been terrific, which is why I could not help but include him in this chapter of Scottish super bosses.

As ambassadors for their country, Stein, Shankly, Busby and Ferguson have been brilliant. Each of them have been honoured by the Queen. Jock became a CBE, Bill was awarded the OBE, Alex has won both the OBE and the CBE, and Matt became Sir Matt Busby CBE. The whole of Britain has paid tribute to these four very special sons of Scotland.

Not Forgetting

THIS HAS to be the most difficult chapter of all. Scotland has produced so many outstanding players. If I wrote a chapter about each one of them then this book would take on the proportions of the world's most famous encyclopaedia. In this effort to pay tribute to as many as possible, I just know that as soon as the book appears on the shelves I shall realise that I have missed out dozens of footballers who really should have been included. No doubt some of you readers will think exactly the same thing. My sincere apologies go to those who have not been mentioned in the book, despite having risen to the top of their profession.

Everyone is someone else's hero, and here are a few more of mine.

Eric Caldow was a fast left-back who gained numerous honours in the 1950s and 1960s as captain of both Scotland and Rangers. He was strong in the tackle and had tremendous vision. He was nothing like the archetypical caveman of a defender, having a quick brain to match those lightning feet.

He won 40 senior caps for Scotland, from 1957 when he made his debut against Spain, to 1963 when his farewell was an extremely painful one. He broke his leg in three places in the 2-1 win over England at Wembley. His international career included the 1958 World Cup, and he even managed four goals which is not bad for a defender.

Eric was a particular hero of mine because he had great fighting spirit as well as tremendous talent. I would have loved to have played alongside him but it was not to be. He is still football daft and goes along to Ibrox regularly.

Jim Delaney made quite a name for himself despite a number of setbacks during his early career. He was quite injury-prone, and was thought to be brittle-boned, which is not exactly ideal for a professional footballer. Once you get that sort of a reputation, many clubs refuse to take a chance on you. Jimmy did not give up, however, and eventually proved to be one of the best forwards in the game during a career that began in the 1930s and did not finish until the 1950s.

Jimmy was equally at home as centre-forward or right winger, but it is probably on the wing that he was at his best. He made 13 appearances for Scotland from 1936 to 1948, with a few wartime games thrown in as well. On the domestic side of his career, he was famous for wearing the shirts of Celtic, Manchester United and Derry City. He also created something of a record when he won the Scottish Cup with Celtic in 1937, The FA Cup with United in 1948 and the Irish Cup with Derry in 1954. If only he had played in Wales as well, he might have won a complete set of winners' medals.

Bobby Collins was a player I really looked up to as well. What a great little Scotsman he was. He played for Celtic in the early 1950s, and had already gained a collection of medals for both League and Cup successes before moving to England to play for Everton, and then Leeds. It was thought that he was over-the-hill when Leeds signed him, but he proved to be the ace up Don Revie's sleeve and led the side back to the top division in 1964, and to the FA Cup Final in 1965 — playing his heart out even though we were beaten.

It seemed that his career was over when he broke his leg badly in 1965. However, he fought back to fitness at an age when most players would have been ready to hang up their boots. He joined Bury and led them to promotion in 1968. As a Scotland player he was among the regulars from 1951 to 1965, and won a total of 31 caps. He richly deserved his Footballer of the Year award in 1965 and was, for me, one of the most inspiring players I have ever known. It was an honour to be in the same Leeds side and I was thrilled that, when I made my senior debut for Scotland, Bobby Collins was in the team. He was a tremendous player and a great help to me in my early days.

Willie Bauld might not have earned as many Scotland caps as most of my other heroes but what a player he was. He scored in two of his three appearances for his country and I am surprised that he did not win a lot more caps. Willie was one of the Edinburgh brigade and made his name with Hearts as a member of their highly successful side of the 1950s.

With Willie as inside forward, Hearts won the Scottish Cup and were twice champions of Scotland, which earned them the right to do battle in the European Cup. To this day, Willie is still their top scorer in that competition, having scored twice against Standard Liege in the 1958-59 campaign.

Willie Bauld is remembered as a brilliantly clever inside-forward with fast footwork, great passing ability and the strength to keep running all day if necessary. He knew where the goal was as well, scoring a hat-trick in the 1956 Scottish Cup Final in which Hearts beat Motherwell 4-2. He whacked in another two in the 1959 Scottish League Cup Final, when Partick were the victims of a 5-1 defeat. In the Hearts Hall of Fame, Willie Bauld is one of the star names.

Bill Brown is another legendary figure in my list of Scottish soccer heroes. He is one of the few international stars to have made his senior debut for his country during a World Cup tournament. His first game was against France during the 1958 World Cup, and he was still playing for Scotland when I made my debut in 1965. In fact, his 28 caps were quite spread out, his last coming against Italy in November 1965. At a time when the English press seemed to delight in telling us that our goalkeepers were no good, Bill returned what I think are reasonable figures — with 41 goals going past him, while his team-mates were scoring 73 at the other end.

Possibly, if Bill had remained in Scotland throughout his career, he might have won even more caps but, as it was, he moved from Dundee in June 1959 and joined Tottenham, where he remained until October 1966. He then joined Northampton for a while. If Bill did miss out on more Scotland caps because of moving to England, he certainly made a wise move in terms of domestic honours since he was a part of the most famous Tottenham team of all time.

The Spurs side of the 1960-61 season was the first this century to win the League championship and FA Cup double in England. In 1962 they again won the FA Cup, and that led to them taking part in the European Cup-winners' Cup competition. In a thrilling Final in May 1963 they beat Atletico Madrid 5-1 in Rotterdam, to become the first British club to win that trophy. It had been quite a competition for Tottenham who had scored 24 goals in four rounds.

By the time that he took off his gloves for the last time, Bill Brown had collected some memorable medals and had ensured a place for himself among both Scotland's and Tottenham's heroes.

Martin Buchan ranks as a hero on both sides of the border as well. His father, Martin senior, had played for Aberdeen and Dundee United just after the last war and coached both Martin junior and his brother George — who also made a name for himself in the game. It was the start of an amazing career that could not possibly be overlooked here.

At 15, Martin had already proved to be a winner. He passed four different A level exams at school and was the star of junior soccer in his area. In October 1966 he made his first-team debut for Aberdeen against Dunfermline and began a tremendous career. There was an interruption early in 1968 when he broke his ankle in a car crash but, within 11 weeks, he was playing in the reserves, and not long after that he was back in the first team again.

In February 1970, at the age of 20, he became Aberdeen's youngest-ever captain and, by April of that same year — now just 21, he led them to a win over Celtic in the Scottish Cup Final. He was a natural choice as skipper of the Scotland under-23 side and, by the end of the 1970-71 season, he had been named Scotland's Player of the Year. The following November he made his first senior appearance for Scotland, and he went on to collect a total of 34 caps which included

World Cup tournaments in 1974 and 1978. During his early international days we were team-mates and you could see then what a great player he was. You would never think that he was such a young man — he played with all the instincts and composure of someone who had been around for years.

Manchester United bought him in March 1972 and he hit the headlines once again. The £125,000 was not only a record for Manchester United, but also a record for a Scottish player. He was also United manager Frank O'Farrell's first major signing — bought as a steadying influence when the side was going through a confidence crisis as their championship form slumped. His debut was an away match at White Hart Lane which United lost but, by the time he had made his first home debut, he had been made captain.

He captained Manchester United to the FA Cup in 1977, beating Liverpool in the Final, and thus became the first player to captain FA Cup-winning sides on both sides of the border. In 1983 he transferred to Oldham as his career entered its twilight zone, but he will always be remembered as a tremendous player and captain for two of the biggest clubs in Britain and a great servant to his country.

In 1978 Kenny Burns won League championship and League Cup winners' medals under Brian Clough at Nottingham Forest. He was also named Footballer of the Year. The following season the League Cup was won again and, more importantly, so was the European Cup in a 1-0 victory over Malmo in Munich. Forest were in the competition again the following season and Kenny picked up another medal when they beat Hamburg 1-0 in Madrid to retain the trophy.

Having begun his Scotland senior career in 1974 when he was with Birmingham, Kenny, a Glasgow-born defender, went on to make a total of 20 appearances, which included the 1978 World Cup in Argentina. He was one of those players who could be relied upon when the going got tough and, because of that, he earned quite a fan following among those who admired his big-hearted style of going in without hesitation when the boots were flying at their hardest.

Kenny played for my old club, Leeds, for a couple of seasons, and then had spells with Derby County, Notts County and Barnsley. He was a gutsy player and a great character throughout his memorable career and he certainly earned his showcase full of honours.

Jimmy Cowan was an excellent goalkeeper who put Morton on the map by becoming their most-capped player — a club record of 25 caps for Scotland. That record still stands today, a fitting memory to a class player who regrettably died in 1968 at the age of 42.

Cowan was a Paisley-born lad who never dreamed that one day he would be keeping goal for Scotland. He wanted to score rather than save goals and he actually began his career as a centre-forward. He was good at it too but, after one or two good displays in goal, it was obvious that he was destined to be stationed between the sticks for the bulk of his career.

He was in goal for Morton during the late 1940s and early 1950s before being sold to Sunderland in June 1953 for £8,000 — which was quite a lot of money for a goalkeeper in those days. His better days had been with Morton though and, of course, with Scotland. The first of Cowan's 25 caps was in 1948 in a 2-0 win over Belgium in Glasgow. He was on the losing side only seven times in all those 25 games, and there was a match to remember in April 1949. It was when Scotland beat England 3-1 at Wembley and Jimmy was chaired off the pitch by his team-mates after a brilliant display in the Scotland goal.

Jimmy Cowan was carved from the sort of Scottish granite reserved for heroes. He was well worthy of this salute.

Charlie Cooke was almost a reluctant hero. A brilliantly talented player, he had no illusions about himself and the reason why he was a professional player. He was a star both in Scotland and in England but refused to take himself seriously, despite so often being hailed as another George Best.

Charlie was a Fife-born lad who went through the usual stages of schools and district soccer before joining Aberdeen — almost by accident. His pal, Jim Geddes, signed for the Dons and, while he was being watched by them, Charlie was also spotted. Only a few days off his 17th birthday, Charlie Cooke signed on the dotted line for Aberdeen, and thus began a career that was quite spectacular.

At Aberdeen he developed his skills as an outstanding ball-player, but a difference of opinion with manager Tommy Pearson ended with him being made available in 1964. Rangers were first to show an interest but they did not want to spend the £20,000 Aberdeen had placed on his head. Celtic were also keen but took too long to make up their minds. Dundee boss, Bob Shankly, dived in with £40,000 and signed him there and then.

Charlie had a useful couple of seasons with Dundee and made his international debut during his second season with them. His first Scotland game was a 4-1 win over Wales in

November 1965. I missed that game but we were team-mates for a number of others. Charlie was playing in my last game for Scotland and played in just one more after that, taking his total to 16.

In 1966 Dundee made a fair profit when they sold Charlie to Chelsea where Tommy Docherty was then in charge — and that heralded a part of his career that was pure showbusiness. Chelsea were a big profile club with a huge following of trendy celebrities. In the following seasons, Charlie Cooke collected runners-up medals in both the FA Cup and the League Cup, and winners' medals in the FA Cup and the European Cup-winners' Cup. Before ending his career Charlie had a spell with Crystal Palace before returning to Chelsea for his swan-song.

I liked Charlie Cooke because he was a magical player and. despite all the publicity that surrounded him, he kept his feet firmly on the ground. Just to give you some idea, this is how he once described his role in life.

"I'm one of the most selfish people alive but when I'm out there I am not doing it for personal glory. I'm not doing it for money to keep the wolf from the door. I'm not doing it for a 50,000 crowd. I'm doing it so that a handful of people who I really respect can hold their heads high in a pub when they say — 'Yes, I know Charlie Cooke!' ".

Yes, I too knew Charlie Cooke.

We come to another of today's heroes now as we pay tribute to John Collins. John went to Monaco at the end of 1995-96 season, but before that he had become a ray of sunshine piercing the black clouds which had gathered over Celtic for a number of seasons.

Born in Galashiels, John Collins began with Celtic Boys and played for them until his dad broke a leg and could not drive him to the games. That led to John joining Hutchison Vale Boys' Club, and that also meant that instead of going straight into a career with Celtic he actually began with Hibs. It was not a bad thing though as John gained a lot of experience with the Hibees and made his way into the international set-up — first of all at under-21 level and then finally into the senior side. His full Scotland debut was in February 1988 against Saudi Arabia in Riyadh. The result was a 2-2 draw, but it was particularly memorable because John scored on his debut.

What Celtic might have had for nothing they eventually had to pay a record fee for. John finally joined them in July 1990 for £925,000. He had a terrific run with them, even though trophies were hard to come by. Some of his goals were nothing short of breathtaking and it is no wonder that he topped the scoring charts so often.

Having played a major part in the Celtic revival, John Collins wanted to experience the benefits of playing abroad — which is why he left for Monaco in 1996. His heart, however, remains in Scotland and, even if he is not back by the time this book is published, I am sure that we shall see him in action in Scottish domestic football again before he finishes his career. Until then we must simply enjoy his international appearances, which are frequent and will eventually earn him a place in the Scottish FA's Hall of Fame.

Collins is an opportunist with a quick brain. He can pass a ball brilliantly and has a tremendous shot that has broken the heart of many an experienced goalkeeper. He is totally unflappable, the sort of player that any manager would want in his side. In short he is quite a hero.

Tommy Docherty has a reputation as one of the game's great characters. His ready wit and huge personality have made him a legend, but perhaps few people realise that he was also an outstanding player who made 25 appearances for Scotland during the 1950s.

It was November 1949 when Tommy Docherty arrived in England after Preston had paid £4,000 for him as a replacement for Bill Shankly. He had already made his name with Celtic, the team he had supported since childhood, but now he was about to embark on a new phase of his soccer life — one which would make him a huge star south of the border.

As a forceful half-back, Tommy made an instant impact at Preston and helped to arrest their decline. He led them to the Second Division championship and the 1954 FA Cup Final — in which they were beaten by West Brom. Arsenal later signed him in August 1958 and, after a couple of seasons with the Gunners, he transferred to Chelsea where he eventually became coach and then manager.

The list of teams that he later managed is quite amazing, and includes Manchester United, Aston Villa, Wolves, Derby, Preston, Queens Park Rangers and quite a few others. He was successful too and I think that, but for personal problems, he might have turned out to have been one of Manchester United's best managers since Matt Busby.

He was a man's man. In training he was hard, very hard. But he gave back to his players just as much as he expected from them. I thought that he was a little unlucky when it came to taking over as manager of Scotland, which he did in 1971 for a season as caretaker. His record in charge was seven wins out of 12 and only three defeats. The reason that I say he was unlucky was because he did the job at a time when many Scotland regulars were unavailable due to injury or club commitments. It would have been interesting to have seen what he could do with everyone at his disposal.

Tommy Docherty always gave his all, both as a player and as a manager. He still does the same in his capacity as a much-in-demand after-dinner speaker. Nobody sleeps while Tommy is performing.

Willie Donachie is another Glasgow lad who made good. He headed south to start his career, joining Manchester City as a junior before making the grade at Maine Road in the late 1960s. His first team debut was during the 1969-70 season, and he remained with the club for ten years through various ups and downs before moving on to Norwich, Burnley and Oldham — with two sessions with Portland Timbers in between.

In 1976 he won the League Cup with Manchester City, but few other medals came his way — which is a shame really because he was an exceptional left-back, as he proved in his many international appearances for Scotland.

After winning his spurs with his country's under-23 side, Willie made his full debut against Peru in Glasgow in April 1972. He started with a 2-0 victory. His international career continued until November 1978 when he bowed out against Portugal with 35 full caps to his credit, and the experience of having taken part in the 1978 World Cup in Argentina.

Maybe Willie could have done with spending more of his

career with trophy-winning sides. Perhaps then he might have been given the recognition that he really deserved. He was certainly one of the best left-backs that I have ever seen.

Bobby Evans is well-remembered as one of Celtic's greatest midfielders. In the days when Bobby was in his prime there was no such thing as a midfielder. You were a half-back, left, right, or centre. Bobby began as a right-half but later moved to centre. He was another Glaswegian who joined his favourite club and, while with Celtic in the 1950s, he shared in one of their golden spells of success in all three domestic competitions.

After spending so long with Celtic he had a sudden spell of travelling in the latter part of his career. In 1960 he moved to Chelsea and then, during the next few seasons, he played for Newport County, Morton, Third Lanark and Raith Rovers before calling it a day in the mid-1960s.

It was his Scotland career which really captures the imagination as Bobby played 48 times for his country. He began in 1948 with a 3-1 win over Wales, and continued until a defeat in Turkey in June 1960 brought down the curtain on his time as a great servant for the Tartan cause.

Bobby Evans was always very strong in defence and yet retained a marvellous flair for attack that made him an excellent provider for several of Scotland's top scorers. If only there were more heroes like Bobby Evans available today.

Jimmy Gibson was one of those wonderful Wembley Wizards we were talking about earlier. He was a big man who rose to fame with Partick Thistle in the early 1920s and then moved to Aston Villa where he was one of their chief reasons for being so prominent during the 1930s.

Jimmy was first capped when he was with the Jags in 1926 and, surprisingly, made only eight appearances for Scotland. Today he would have been one of the first names on the list for every game. Although he was a big man and a key defender, he was a great ball player and could outshine many an attacker who was supposed to be particularly talented in that sphere of the game.

Much of Gibson's apparent strength was in his great sense of balance. Defenders are often considered to be rather more clumsy than their attacking comrades but, if that is the case, then Jimmy must have been an exception. He had it all — the ability to tackle, the ability to pass and a great talent for beating opponents by the mere shrug of a shoulder or faking a swerve. He was certainly a star.

Bobby Gillespie went down in history as the last amateur player to captain Scotland. He was with Queen's Park for 14 seasons until he quit in 1933, the same year that he was called into the Scotland side as centre-half and captain. He had been called up before — three times in fact — but then he was simply one of the players and not the skipper.

Although he had joined Queen's Park as a centre-forward, he switched to defence and pioneered a new type of defensive play which saw three defenders instead of two. Much of today's strategy in preventing goals goes back to the considerations and play of Bob Gillespie.

What about John Greig? Another man with Rangers written all over him. He had a brilliant career at Ibrox and is still there as a public relations man. You could never imagine Big John having anything to do with any other club. He was with Rangers when he was first capped and stayed there right through his career. He even had a spell as manager, but it did not work out and he is much happier in his present position of spreading the Rangers' message throughout the world.

With Rangers, John won just about every honour possible and has a whole stack of medals in his collection. He was also Scotland's Footballer of the Year twice — in 1966 and 1976 — and it says something for his great career that these great awards were ten years apart. It seemed at one time that he would never actually retire but would just go on playing for ever.

On the international scene, John Greig was fantastic for Scotland. Probably never more so than when Jock Stein was manager of the national side — which is even more special when you consider that Greig was a dyed-in-the-wool Rangers man, and Stein was equally as fervent as a Celtic man. Sportsmen that they were, they never allowed that to get in the way of their common cause — Scotland.

Greig's senior Scotland debut was in April 1964 when England were visitors to Glasgow. His international career began with a victory, a 1-0 win over the Auld Enemy. I can remember that John was in the side when I made my debut in 1965, and we were regular team-mates after that. He was Scotland captain before me, and it was a great honour to take over from him — not just because of skippering my country but because I was following in the boots of such a legend.

Funnily enough, John played one more Scotland game after I had played my last. It was at home to Denmark in October 1975, and once again he was the rock in the centre of the defence as Scotland won 3-1. In all, he had made 44 senior appearances for Scotland. I'm glad to say we are still good pals to this day and John Greig remains, as always, one of my heroes.

It seems appropriate to follow John Greig with a tribute to another great captain and central defender for both Rangers and Scotland — Richard Gough. I'm not going to bore you with all the details of Richard having been born in Sweden and having spent much of his youth in South Africa because, in a sense, that would undermine the fact that he is absolutely 100 per cent Scottish. He would never consider such a thing as playing for either of those other two countries.

Gough has been a tremendous servant to both the Ibrox club and Scotland. He has literally shed blood for both, and has always been an outstanding example to those around him. He began his career with Dundee United, having joined them from Witz University. His first team debut was in itself a baptism of fire as Dundee United took on Celtic in April 1981. The final score was 3-2 to Celtic but it was a tremendous tussle and gave Gough an immediate education into the life and times of Scottish football.

In 1986 he was bought by Tottenham. Life in London, however, did not suit him so well as life in Scotland and, little more than a year after moving to White Hart Lane, he was signed by Rangers. He has been there ever since, skippering them to a phenomenal number of championships and other domestic successes.

Richard Gough's international career came to a sudden halt after a difference of opinion with Andy Roxburgh, but by then he had already earned his place in the Hall of Fame with 61 caps — which have included World Cup and European championship heroics. Had he remained on the international scene, I am sure that Richard Gough would have been a serious challenger to the record 102 caps gained by Kenny Dalglish.

I can pay no greater tribute to Richard Gough than to include him in this book of Scottish heroes and to say that he has been a fantastic player.

An old pal of mine from my Leeds days is Eddie Gray, who may have gained only 12 caps for Scotland — far fewer than the 32 collected by his brother Frank — but was still, in my opinion, a tremendous player who could, and should, have been much more prominent on the international scene.

I was there when he made his Scotland debut in 1969 against England at Wembley. He soon settled into international soccer just as he'd settled when he made his first team debut for Leeds in 1965. He stayed at Elland Road until 1984 and played in 577 senior games. He shared in our triumphs and our disappointments and was a totally reliable player throughout his career.

The Gray family have produced some excellent players and, in naming Eddie in this section, I hope it will also serve as a tribute to all of them.

If it's goals that you're after then you don't have to look much further than Alan Gilzean who hit 12 in his 22 Scotland games and very many more in his club football. He was a tremendous player and goal scorer, absolutely brilliant in the air and he frightened goalkeepers to death every time a cross came into the area.

It was Alan's great goal talent that took Dundee to the Scottish championship in the 1961-62 season, and saw them progress to the semi-finals of the European Cup the following season. There was much more to his game, however, than just scoring goals. He also had this wonderful ability to draw a group of defenders and then send a simple flick to a colleague for them to find the net.

Gilzean joined Spurs in 1964 and played alongside Jimmy Greaves and then Martin Chivers. He was in the FA Cup-winning side of 1967 and also the team which won the UEFA Cup in 1972. Not long after that he left Tottenham after having scored more than 100 goals for them.

There was no more majestic sight than seeing Alan Gilzean soar into the air and head the ball into the net — unless of course you were on the opposing side.

Talking of goals brings us to one of Scotland's top goalkeepers, who is not only a great goalie but is no mean hand at cricket. Yes, of course, it's Andy Goram, famed for his service to his country and to Rangers.

You don't get them much more Scottish than Andy — even if he was born in Bury. His father, Lewis, was also a goalkeeper and played for Berwick and Hibs. Young Andy was on schoolboy terms with West Brom, but they released him and he went along to Bury on the off chance to see if there was any hope for him there. He never found out if there was or not — because he walked out after waiting to see the manager, only to find out that he was finishing a game of snooker first. You didn't mess with Andy Goram, even in those days.

He had better luck at Oldham where Jimmy Frizzell was manager. In May 1982 Andy made his first team debut and kept a clean sheet in a 1-0 win over Charlton. It was quite poetic when, five years later, he joined Hibs and stood between the posts on the same pitch as his father had done some years earlier. Rangers signed him in 1991 and he has been there ever since.

As well as a collection of medals, Andy also has a collection of caps with more than 40 to his credit — and probably a lot more by the time you read this. There will probably be still more yet since Andy has said that he plans to keep going at least until the year that he celebrates his 40th birthday — 2004. Sounds like a lot of goalkeeping heroics still to come and that will delight his many fans both at Ibrox and Hampden.

When he does retire, Andy Goram will probably catch up with his cricket. He has been capped by Scotland in that sport as well and he should still be fit enough to play by the time he quits soccer. Now that's what you call an all-rounder!

Over at Parkhead they still talk about David Hay and the tremendous talent that he brought to the game. He was undoubtedly one of the stars of the 1970s and a great defender for Celtic and later for Chelsea. It was Celtic who gave him his chance and he emerged in the late 1960s to claim a first-team spot with the mighty Celts.

His career blossomed and he was hailed as one of the brightest new talents of the decade by the time the Swinging Sixties had turned into the Scintillating Seventies. His fame spread far beyond Glasgow, which is why Chelsea signed him in August 1974. With both clubs he earned his share of awards and, when he left Stamford Bridge in 1978, he could look back on a career that had been as rewarding as it had been exciting.

David was a tremendous modern defender. He could tackle, and was very quick in that tackle but, equally, he had a speedy recovery, could take the ball, control it, and set off on a run that would have the opposition in a panic. He loved to run at opponents and could take them on with all the finesse of a regular winger. He was courageous and lived for the game as any of his many fans will testify.

His Scotland career began in April 1970 with a 1-0 win over Northern Ireland, and it ended in the 1974 World Cup when we drew with Yugoslavia. In all he collected 27 senior caps and I can only repeat what I said at the time — that David Hay was an outstanding player who could have walked into any team in the world and stayed there.

Let's come bang up to date again in order to salute one of today's great stars. Paul McStay has been a terrific player for Celtic and for Scotland. Of course, the name McStay has been associated with Celtic for some time, since the family has had four other members wearing the green and white in the last 70 years. The whole McStay clan is Celtic daft.

Paul began with Celtic Boys' Club before becoming a full-time professional and making his debut on 23 January 1982. He was only 17 at the time and, in that same year, he was a member of the Scottish Youth team that won the European championship. When he made his senior debut for his country in 1984, he was the second youngest-ever cap for Scotland behind Denis Law. No wonder Paul seems to have been around for so long.

He has been through some good and some bad times with Celtic under a succession of managers, and there have been times when he has been tempted to sign for one of the many clubs who have made enquiries. Each time he pulled back from the brink.

"Although I gave it a lot of thought, it would have broken my heart to leave Celtic." He once said. "For me, Celtic are the best and the only club. I would be happy to stay here for ever, even if it was on the turnstiles. The grass could not be greener elsewhere."

Circumstances can necessitate a change of mind of course, but I doubt that there will ever be a change in Paul's heart. Celtic is in his blood. He has won each of the major domestic honours with Celtic, and has an ever-growing haul of Scotland appearances that will eventually make him one of the most-capped Scots of all time. In 1988 he was named Footballer of the Year by both the press and his fellow professionals, five years after he was named the Scottish PFA's Young Player of the Year. You can imagine what his personal trophy cabinet looks like.

What makes him so special? Class, sheer class! He has the lot — the ability to beat players, make terrific passes and score goals. He is a great leader of men and has the respect of everyone in the game. He is everything that a top professional should be.

Alex McLeish. You can't help but get excited when you mention the name. He is one of the greatest defenders that Aberdeen have ever known and has won 77 caps for his country — which puts him among a very elite band indeed ... the top five Scottish international cap winners.

Alex is a master of his trade, commanding in defence, with excellent ability in the air and a great presence on the ground. A big man, he is one of those players who can scare the pants off opponents just by being there. He was born in Glasgow in January 1959 and made a name for himself with

Glasgow United before Aberdeen dived in and stole him from under the noses of the big two.

His first-team debut for the Dons was on 2 January 1978, in a 1-0 win over Dundee United in front of 23,000 fans at Pittodrie. He was just approaching his 19th birthday and his boss, Alex Ferguson, decided to take a gamble on him. It was the start of a run that would see him spend the next 17 seasons at Pittodrie, and share in some of the greatest moments that the club has ever known.

The medals have come thick and fast with championships and cups — including the famous Aberdeen triumph in the European Cup-winners' Cup. He pulled on the Aberdeen shirt for nearly 600 League games plus all those cup matches. He was a part of the furniture at Pittodrie and somehow it was quite appropriate that, when the Dons unveiled their new Richard Donald stand in 1993, Alex was the first to score a goal in front of it. The place erupted and it wasn't just because it was the first goal that he'd scored in three years — it was in salute to a great player.

His Scotland career began in the under-23 side and he made his senior debut in March 1980 in a 4-1 win over Portugal. He experienced the thrills of playing in both the World Cup and European championship tournaments before making his final Scotland appearance in 1993.

In 1994 he finally left Aberdeen and moved to Motherwell to become their player-manager. I am sure that it was the right time for him to enter into a new phase in his career and I believe that he will go on to make his mark as one of the top bosses in the game. He has certainly proved to be one of the best players that we have ever known.

There is another Scot who has recently started a career in management and will, I am sure, make as big a name for himself in that role as he did as a player. There is no doubt that he has been one of the most popular Scottish characters in recent decades and has also made it into the Hall of Fame. I am talking about the Wee Man himself — Gordon Strachan.

Strach has had quite a career, written off several times but always bouncing back for more. He is one of the Edinburgh brigade, having been born there in February 1957. He was a really fiery character when he was a lad and there is the classic story of when he joined his first club, Dundee, and was playing in a reserves team. On the opposite side were twins. One of them fouled Gordon but he didn't know which one — so he punched both of them to make sure that he got the right one.

To call him a character is an understatement, but he's much more than that. He has been a terrific footballer and a great inspiration to all who have had the good fortune to play alongside him. He has also been admired by opponents. As an example, when he was in Dundee's reserves side he was voted Reserves Player of the Year in two successive seasons. This was an award which was given to the player who polled the most votes by opposing managers.

Once he had made his first-team debut in April 1975, there was no stopping him. Dundee beat Hearts 2-0 that day and his reputation soared. After three seasons of first-team football he moved to Aberdeen, the Dons having paid £80,000 for him. Alex Ferguson was his boss there and together they won just about everything that was going in Scotland, as well as the European Cup-winners' Cup and the European Super Cup.

In August 1984 Ron Atkinson paid £500,000 to take the

Wee Man to Manchester United and it was a little ironic that, a couple of years later, he should be joined there by his former boss, Alex Ferguson. He played a major part in the foundations of United's revival under Alex, but a new challenge came in 1989 when he was bought by Leeds for £300,000. He had been a professional for 18 years but it was as if he were starting all over again.

To Howard Wilkinson's Leeds side, Strach brought an extra dimension of class, experience and vision. He engineered their rise to the top division and then their success in winning the last First Division championship before the birth of the Premiership. He had become a player's player, a confidence giver who could create goals from nothing. His sense of humour became legend and he had turned from being a one-time bad boy into a fan pleaser.

Several times it looked as though injury had finished his career — but he always bounced back again and seemed to get better and better. He announced his retirement from playing and the commencement of his full-time coaching career. Then he joined Coventry in March 1995 and started playing again. Ron Atkinson was the man who took him to Highfield Road and when Ron moved 'upstairs' to an executive position, it was Gordon who became team manager. He still pulled on the shirt and I can see him turning out, even ten years from now, if there is a need.

Strachan's Scotland performances have won him 50 caps and a wealth of experience. I have a vision of him being Scotland manager one day and if it happens you can expect to see our national side playing with fire in their bellies and smiles on their faces.

Joe Jordan was a fearsome goal scorer in his day. A son of Carluke, he began his career with Morton but he was quickly snapped up by Leeds, who paid a bargain £15,000 for him in 1971. He soon became a popular figure with the Leeds fans — and with us, the players. He was fearless and would chase anything in the box, regardless of how high or how hard the boots were flying. He was also fantastic in the air, and many of his greatest goals — and there were plenty of them — came from his head.

It was a shock to the Elland Road fans when Manchester United boss, Dave Sexton, signed him in January 1978 for £350,000. Leeds had certainly made a profit from him — and not just in terms of money. He had made a great contribution to the club's successes during his time there.

He soon won over the Old Trafford fans as well and continued to score some great goals. When Sexton left the club several players soon departed also. Joe was among them and he went to AC Milan for £175,000 where he proved to be just as popular with the Italian fans who loved his rugged style. Later he played for Verona, Southampton and Bristol City, before going into management. He has been boss of Hearts and Stoke as well as having two spells with Bristol City.

Joe played 52 times for Scotland and scored 11 goals, which put him among our top ten hit-men. To me, there was no finer sight than seeing the ball come across from the wing and watching the head of Joe Jordan rising majestically above all the others to nod it into the net.

There are any amount of other names to be remembered. Just think of the skills of John Robertson who picked up 28

Scottish caps during his career with Nottingham Forest and Derby during the mid-1970s to the mid-1980s. My old pal, Peter Lorimer, collected 21 caps and was also a great servant to Leeds. We were team-mates for a number of years and had some happy and successful times, both at Elland Road and in Scotland colours.

Sandy Jardine played 38 times for Scotland and was another of the great Rangers stalwarts of the 1970s and early 1980s. Bobby Murdoch was brilliant for Celtic and shared in their great European glory in 1967, but let's not forget that he also played 12 times for his country — and never had a bad game. Steve Nicol is still going strong and can reflect on a great career, both at club level with Liverpool and in 27 appearances for Scotland. Pat Nevin is also still in the frame and has been a valuable asset to Scotland and his various clubs — which have included Chelsea, Everton and Tranmere. David Narey played 35 times for his country from 1977 to 1989, and the Dundee fans will tell you that he is one of the best players ever to wear their shirt.

Alan Rough played 56 times between the sticks for Scotland, most of his caps coming during his great days with Partick Thistle, his last appearances being made while he was with Hibernian. Who could forget the great performances of Asa Hartford or Maurice Malpas, or the excitement of seeing Ian St John in full flow — contributing nine goals in 21 games for his country, and countless more for Motherwell and Liverpool.

Digging a little deeper into the history of Scottish football, what about the great Alex James of baggy shorts fame? During the heady days of Arsenal's triumphs in the 1930s, Alex was vital to their cause, a genius of an inside-forward who linked defence and attack like high-quality oil — keeping the engine running smoothly. He won only eight caps, but his role in the Wembley Wizards side earned him a place among the heroes.

Willie Woodburn was a dominating centre-half who won 24 caps, five Scottish championship medals, four Scottish Cup medals and two Scottish League Cup medals. He was a hero at Ibrox in the late 1930s and well into the 1950s. His indefinite ban in 1954 for disciplinary offences — lifted three years later — could never blot out his great career as a top professional footballer.

The great Liverpool favourite of the immediate post-war period was Billy Liddell — and why not? He played 28 times for Scotland and — a club record — 492 League games for the Reds. He was fantastic with both feet, could shoot from any range and was terrific with his head. He was one of those players who could turn out in any forward position and give you a great performance.

Ian McColl played 14 times for Scotland, and later became manager while he was still a player with Rangers in 1960. He held the job for four and a half years and won 16 of his 27 matches. Probably he is best remembered in the Rangers shirt, which he wore more than 600 times in 15 years at Ibrox. He collected seven championship medals and five cup medals, and was a great right-half in the Rangers line-up that became known as the 'Iron Curtain' because it was such a tight defence.

If you like goal scorers, look no further than Jimmy McCrory, who only played three times for Scotland but had a fantastic club record with Celtic. He scored 550 goals in his first-class career between the two World Wars. In British League football, he is the only player to have averaged a goal a game during his career. In 1928 he put eight past Dunfermline in one game, and in 1936 he scored four in five minutes against Motherwell. What price would he carry today?

We mentioned Alan Morton — the 'Wee Blue Devil' — in the chapter on the Wembley Wizards. He had a great Rangers partnership with Bob McPhail, who scored 281 goals in 466 games for Rangers. Many of those goals came from play set up by Morton. There were M & Ms at Ibrox even in those days.

Tommy Walker is one of the all-time greats of Hearts. Not only was he a terrific inside-forward during the 1930s, but as manager of the club later on, he produced such fantastic talent as Dave Mackay and Alex Young. He also guided Hearts to the championship twice, and the Scottish Cup and the League Cup four times. He also chalked up 20 appearances for Scotland in what was a really glittering career.

Who was nicknamed 'Scotland's Stanley Matthews'? It sounds like a pub trivia quiz question doesn't it? The answer is Gordon Smith, who was a wizard on the wing in the immediate post-war period and won 18 caps between 1946 and 1957. He was a tremendously skilful player for Hibs and Dundee and he thoroughly deserved being rated alongside the mighty Matthews.

Bobby Templeton is a real blast from the past. He played for Scotland 11 times at the turn of the century, and played his club football for Aston Villa, Newcastle, Woolwich Arsenal and Kilmarnock. He was an amazing left winger who had breathtaking ball skills and could also pinpoint a pass, with such precision it was said, that he could land the ball on a postage stamp from the other side of the pitch. Templeton was also said to be 'wayward'– sometimes a problem with those described as a 'genius'. There's nothing new, is there?

Billy Steel made such an impact on his international debut in April 1947, that a month later he was picked to play for Great Britain against the Rest of Europe. Morton sold him to Derby for a British record £15,000 but, in 1950, he returned to Scotland and Dundee and then in 1954, having won 30 caps, he suddenly took off for America, leaving behind him a brief but spectacular soccer career.

We could go on and on naming the names but, however many I can think of, there are sure to be others that are forgotten. There are three more that I have deliberately left out so far but I am going to put that right without further delay.

First of all, I should like to pay tribute to John Thomson. At the end of the 1920s he emerged as one of Scotland's most promising goalkeepers. At the age of 22 he had played four times for Scotland and had established himself as Celtic's first choice goalie. He had already helped them to two championships and there was the potential of many more honours still to come.

John's mother once had a dream that he would be badly injured during a game and it was a constant worry to her that, one day, her dream might come true. Tragically, it did! He was playing in a Rangers-Celtic match on 5 September 1931. The second half was just five minutes old when he went for a 50-50 ball with Sam English. The collision between the two left John unconscious on the ground with blood seeping from his ear. He was immediately stretchered off and taken to hospital. He never regained consciousness and died at 9.25 that night.

His courage and athleticism proved to be John's undoing. There was never any question of foul play and Sam English lived with that tragic accident for the rest of his life. It seems appropriate somehow to pay a belated tribute to John Thomson — a real hero.

There was another tragedy in the death of the brilliant John White. John's career had begun with Falkirk in the latter half of the 1950s and his international career began while he was still there, starring in a 4-0 victory over Northern Ireland in Belfast in 1959. Spurs manager, Bill Nicholson, had seen him and Dave Mackay added to the recommendation. Just a few days after that match, White became a Spurs player.

He had never been to London before in his life, but he quickly adapted to life in the capital and played a major part in the magnificent Tottenham side which rewrote the history books in the early 1960s. By the end of the 1964 season he had everything going for him. He had played 22 games for Scotland and was hailed as being one of the best players seen in the Football League for years. He was still only 26 and had a lovely wife, a two-year-old daughter and a six-month-old son.

His death came on a golf course in July 1964 when he was struck by lightning. The whole of the football world was shocked and there were moving scenes at his funeral a few days later. I believe that John White would have gone on to become even more of a legend. I hope that this tribute helps his family to keep their heads high as we join in remembering him as a son of Scotland — a great hero.

Neither of these two greats that I have just mentioned would want us to finish this chapter on a sombre note and so I have left until last another of the game's great characters. He is a man who has had both the bouquets and the brickbats. He has lived through nightmares on the pitch and been harangued off it. However, he has still bounced back for more and, as I write this, it looks as if he has every chance of playing in the 1998 World Cup. At one time things were going so horribly wrong in his career that he nearly gave up. His family talked him out of it and he has stormed back to become a Scotland international once again.

For sheer bravery, both on and off the pitch, I have to say that this man thoroughly deserves the success he has enjoyed as his career has entered its second phase. He was terrific with Aberdeen, brilliant with Manchester United, and then suffered because of a few mistakes made under the glare of television cameras. His confidence was shattered and nobody would give him a real chance except for a few loan spells.

A return to Scotland changed all of that. He regained some respect during a couple of years with Dundee and then stormed back to such form with Hibernian that he was recalled to the Scotland side where he performed such heroics to keep his team on the road to France in 1998. I was really pleased for him and as it adds to his record collection of Scotland caps — the most awarded to a Scottish goalkeeper — I am delighted to say you are a hero to ...Jim Leighton.

In a moment we shall turn our attention to the potential heroes of tomorrow but, before then, let's just look back again and reflect on these great names of yesterday and today. They have worn the badge with honour and Scotland can be rightly proud of them. Through them, football has been enriched — both at home and throughout the world. They have fought against the odds and won, they have smashed through the barriers of physical pain and mental despair too. That's the stuff that makes real heroes — Scottish heroes.

The Dream Team

THIS IS THE chance that everyone would like — to pick a Dream Team to take on all-comers. It gives you an opportunity to indulge yourself and to create a few arguments too! It goes without saying that whatever team I might pick, it will be disputed. How could he leave out so-and-so? What's wrong with what's-his-name? He must be mad to leave out old George — he was the best ever!

All managers have that kind of conversation ringing in their ears all the time. You get used to it after a while. You have to, because your job hinges on the decisions you personally take and, if you allow other people to pick your team for you, you might just as well pack it all in.

One of the good things about the Fantasy Leagues that have been so popular in recent years is that it shows just how difficult it can be to pick a team capable of winning week in and week out. A manager's lot is not always a happy one, but I am determined to enjoy mine as I select, what I believe to be, the best Scotland side of all time.

In picking my Dream Team for Scotland I have put myself on the bench but, I have to say, it would be tempting to get on the park for at least a few minutes, just to be able to say that I had played in the greatest Scottish international of all time. What do you think of this for a team that the Tartan Army could follow with pride?

In goal I have gone for Jimmy Cowan. I expect that most of you thought that I would go for Andy Goram or one of the other goalie greats, but Jimmy always seemed to me to be the one who would get the nod before all the others. He gave tremendous confidence to any team in which he played and he always employed skills that were safe rather than spectacular. Jimmy could fly across the face of the goal and tip the ball round a post, or over the bar, just like the best of the rest — but he had that extra something too, that made him one of the most imposing last lines of defence that might ever be found on a soccer pitch. Yes, Jimmy Cowan gets the No 1 jersey. He was outstanding in the 1948-49 season and, in the Wembley international against England that season, he virtually beat them all on his own. That's my kind of goalkeeper.

Who get's the No 2 shirt? I thought about all of my choices for quite some time and I finished up with a short list that was not quite so short for the right-back spot. I did keep coming back to the same name though — a player who was just superb in that position. He did a fantastic job for Celtic and for Scotland — rugged in the tackle, quick to get an attack going and a heart as strong as an ox. He is, of course, the legendary Danny McGrain.

To link up with him there would have to be a left-back

with a similar style and equal talent, and that's why I've chosen a Rangers man who impressed everyone whether friend or foe. He could read a game tremendously, plotting each move by his opponents long before it happened. I know he would have an instant rapport with Danny McGrain and that is exactly what is needed among defenders. As well as talking to each other, players have to be on the same mental wavelength — and that's why Eric Caldow gets to line up with Danny McGrain as my Dream Team full-backs.

Let's have a look at the central defenders next. Again there are many great names who spring to mind, but I'm going to pick two more legends who would get on well and provide a solid wall in the centre of the park. The first is a Celtic man who hardly missed anything in the air. He was fantastic to watch as he plucked out one high ball after another. He was a rock and would be just the job for such a class side. I am talking about Celtic's fantastic captain, Billy McNeill, who never failed to perform well and show outstanding leadership qualities.

Alongside Billy would have to be the player's player, a Scotsman who not only had tremendous ability but also amazing courage. For anybody to come back from injury the way he came back is quite something, and his never-give-up attitude is certainly something that I would want in my team. He was simply brilliant in every team in which he played and, as I have said before, I wonder if the supporters really appreciated just how good he really was. A great, great player, Dave Mackay could not be left out.

Providing midfield thrust, I have gone for two players who were completely different in style. One was a total extrovert who had the most incredible skills and knew it. He loved beating players and setting up his team-mates for goals that were almost made easy by his tremendous ability to put them in just the right place at the right time. He enjoyed making defenders squirm, especially if they were wearing an England shirt. Yes, that's right, I'm going for Jim Baxter as one of my midfielders.

Alongside him I have decided upon a player who was possibly underrated. He was known to be hard in the tackle, but there was much more to his game than that. He was a ball-player and had great vision. He did not shirk a challenge and could sometimes be a little volatile. Make no mistake, he was a very, very good footballer and was a constructive player as much as he was destructive to opposition attacks. Take your place Graeme Souness.

We have our goalkeeper, our defence and our midfield. I like to see wingers in full use and I am picking my Dream Team with that in mind. I believe that I shall be picking a couple of players who very rarely featured on the same side — only once, if my memory and research is correct. I still cannot understand this and, really, it seems to be another case of Scotland shooting ourselves in the foot by not giving proper thought to the selection.

On the right, playing as an orthodox winger, I would place Jimmy Johnstone. His hypnotic skills and electrifying pace would keep the forwards bubbling for the entire 90 minutes. As I mentioned earlier, he was one of those players who you wanted to give the ball to — just to watch what he would do with it. I believe that he would be fantastic on the right wing. He could play with either foot, so it would be no problem to him wherever he played.

No prizes for guessing who would be on the left flank. I have already given the game away so, without any hesitation, let us hand Willie Henderson his shirt. With Jimmy on the other side of the pitch, leaving defenders stranded, and pumping crosses in for the goalscorers, Willie would have the same sort of freedom to demonstrate that aspect of his game, while also having the the sort of opportunity he loved — namely, to cut inside and go for goal himself. Playing that way we would have the option of winger, or third hit-man.

There are only two other places in the starting line-up, and those are for the guys who have to put the ball into the back of the net. It is almost a foregone conclusion who they might be. When the two top Scottish scorers are available to you it would be ridiculous not to use them. I would have Kenny Dalglish slightly behind his strike partner, because Kenny was also so very good at drawing defenders and setting up other players to add the finishing touch. If a side left him unmarked, or unchallenged, they were always punished for it — so I do not think that any opponents that my Dream Team might face would dare to leave him unshackled for long, and that in itself would create problems for them because Kenny was a master at giving defenders the slip.

Slightly in front of Kenny, with the task of hitting the most goals, would be the Lawman — the maned gunslinger with 30 Scottish notches on his boots. With Jimmy, Willie, Jim and Kenny supplying, Denis Law would have the time of his life. I can see that raised arm and big grin as one goal after another goes up on the scoreboard. Denis was born to score goals and his record shows that he fulfilled his potential. On the ground, up in the air or halfway between for a side-on volley, they were all chances for Denis — and he never failed to try every one. His strike rate was amazing and that's why he has to be in the Dream Team.

We are allowed substitutes and, while I would really like to be among the five on the bench, I suppose I would simply have to sit there as manager, wishing that someone else had picked the Dream Team and I could be lucky enough to be among their choices.

Despite what everyone else says, Scotland has produced some great goalkeepers, and there would be little problem in picking a substitute cover for Jimmy Cowan. My vote would be marginally in favour of Andy Goram, although it would be hard to disappoint a player like Jim Leighton and several more. Alex McLeish gets my vote to cover for defence to midfield. He could be drafted into just about any position in an emergency, either as full-back, central defender or in midfield. Alex would have no problem in coping with any of those positions.

I need another substitute for the same role, someone who could fit into any of the defensive or midfield positions — and possibly even go into attack if it was really necessary. I could not think of anyone better than Willie Miller to slot into that place and, if he was sent on for Billy McNeill, he might find himself getting the captain's armband as well.

There are still two places on the subs' bench, and I have picked two men who would not only give their all on the pitch, but would also be invaluable in the dressing-room in keeping up the team's spirit. They are two of the game's great personalities. One is the Wee man, Gordon Strachan. Gordon is just the sort of player to send on when the legs start to tire.

His pace and enthusiasm have often lifted a side just when they are beginning to flag. He is another of those utility players who could perform equally well in a midfield or an attacking role — and I would not put it past him to take over as centre-half if there was a need, all 5ft 6ins of him.

My final substitute has quite a reputation for hitting all-important goals late in the game. When he came back after a lengthy injury and sat on the Scotland bench against Greece in 1995, he could not wait to get involved in the game. In the 72nd minute he was given his chance with the score still at 0-0. In less than a minute after getting on to the park, he scored what proved to be the only goal of the game. With that sort of ability and a fantastic scoring record to his credit, Ally McCoist would have to be on the bench.

So there you have it, my Dream Team, lining up like this:

Cowan

McGrain   **McNeill**   **Mackay**   **Caldow**

Souness   **Baxter**

Johnstone   **Dalglish**   **Law**   **Henderson**

Subs: *Goram, McLeish, Miller, Strachan, McCoist*.

What price this lot against the Auld Enemy!?

Why I Fear
for the Future

WHAT of the heroes of tomorrow? Will there be any? Yes, of course there will, but I do have fears for the Scottish game and its future — and, indeed, for those heroes to come. They might be lauded at home, but what about the world stage? There is a real danger that Scottish football is going nowhere — fast!

Scotland has always produced people with natural flair and passion, whatever their walk of life. Football has often highlighted that fact. The skills have been there for all to see and that passion has seen Scotland out of many a tight corner. But is the passion enough if the skills are being stifled?

I believe that we have become very mechanical in our approach to the game. It was a breath of fresh air to me when I went to last year's Scottish Coca-Cola Cup Final and saw Hearts using real wingers who had been given the freedom to use their abilities. They had not been shackled to a tight game plan, and the result was a highly entertaining and exciting game of football. Okay! So they lost to Rangers, 3-2 — but they were able to come off that pitch with their heads held high, and on another day the scoreline could just as easily have been in their favour.

The game in Scotland is lacking something and it shows in our national team. I think that we have done brilliantly to get so many World Cup finals and European Championships — even as I write this it seems there is a good chance that we shall be among the elite again in France in the 1998 World Cup. In recent years, however, I have often wondered how we have actually gained the results that — on paper at least — have spelled success.

I have come to the conclusion that we have won through by determination, desire, and a reasonable slice of luck. We are only a small country and we have done well to figure so often in the major competitions but, nevertheless, I cannot help but feel that these days we are getting there with less skill.

To back up my point, the home World Cup qualifier against Sweden was a classic example. I was at that game and I was delighted that we won but, to be honest, The Swedish team could have swamped us to the tune of 5-0. They went away in total disbelief that they had actually lost and I couldn't blame them.

Don't get me wrong! I am as thrilled as anybody when Scotland win — no matter how well or badly we have played. What I am saying is that we cannot rely upon luck — or other teams not being able to get the ball into the net because we have a goalkeeper on form — or that their forwards have forgotten where to find the goal.

We have to safeguard the future of our game, the future of

football in Scotland, and I do not think that we are really doing that at the moment. It will prove to be our undoing in the future.

Let us examine football in Scotland as we find it today. Money rules everything and is creating all kinds of pressures that are damaging the game. Club managers are constantly under pressure to get instant results. There is very little building for the future because the managers are not allowed to look into the future. Why?

The reason that managers are under pressure is because too much is expected too quickly. The supporters are encouraged to be impatient. They are encouraged to take part in these various radio phone-ins and give the manager and the board some stick. The more the fans moan, the better the radio presenters like it because it creates controversy and gets them more listeners. Many radio presenters angle their questions to get the fans to have a real go at the people running the clubs.

It doesn't stop there of course. Today we also have TV and radio pundits who are quick to have a go at managers just so that they can enhance their own reputations for so-called 'straight-talking'. All this serves to do is create panic in the boardroom and lower the axe over the manager's head. He has to get instant results to stave off execution. One way is to throw up a defensive wall and turn his players into robots so that they give nothing away. An alternative is to buy in other players.

Where can he buy players here? The chances are that most managers do not have time to bring on players from lower divisions or non-League soccer, so they buy from outside

Scotland. The two most prominent teams in Scotland — Rangers and Celtic — are prime examples of this. Yes, of course, it is good to see the skills of these players, but it is killing our game. Bringing in foreign players by choice is the short-term answer. In the long term it is stopping the development of talent from within the country. If teams are spending huge amounts of money on imports then they have less to spend on the development of home-grown talent.

Not too long ago it was accepted that many Scottish youngsters would go to English clubs at the start of their careers. Some would stay, but many would filter back from the Manchester Uniteds and their youth schemes and go on to enjoy successful careers in Scottish soccer. Even if they were rejected by a major club in England they had still received a good grounding, good enough to land them a better job with one of the top clubs in Scotland. What we see happening now is very few Scottish lads getting any experience at all in England — or even with a major Scottish club. As a result most of them are destined to part-time football in the lower divisions of the Scottish League — that is, if they are lucky.

I am not saying that the answer to everything is to play in England, but it certainly did me no harm and when you look at players like Denis Law, Kenny Dalglish, Jim Leighton, Richard Gough, Bill Shankly, Matt Busby, Tommy Docherty, Graeme Souness, Alan Hansen and others, you see stars who have obviously benefited from playing in English soccer. That is not happening now because Scotland is not producing that kind of talent.

Another problem with having too many foreign players in your competition is that you start to lose a sense of identity.

When the Americans tried to get soccer going on a major scale some years ago, they failed miserably. It was nothing to do with a lack of interest in the game because there were certainly big crowds turning out at the start. It was the simple fact that all the players were foreigners. There was not one American among them and that really killed off interest. In trying again, the Americans have taken a long, hard look at what went wrong. Before launching their new competition they have worked extremely hard at getting schools interested and starting coaching camps all over the country. They began developing the young talent before even beginning to develop the professional set-up.

I feel sorry for people like Craig Brown. As national team manager he is totally dependent on clubs producing the young players who can eventually be called up to represent their country. If the clubs do not have good youth football and proper coaching, the national team manager has no chance of doing anything other than survive. It is a great achievement to get to the finals of a major tournament these days — but it is getting even harder simply because our soccer is lacking an interest in tomorrow.

This blinkered approach that Scottish football is enduring at the moment is little short of a suicide bid. I know that things go in cycles and therefore I hope that this is just a phase that we are going through — unfortunately, I do not believe it is!

We must give the game back to the people who have made it. The accountants are ruling everything at the moment. When the game finishes up lying in tatters, they will simply go off to ruin something else. Football is a very simple game which is there to be enjoyed and I believe that a lot more should be done to help players, managers and supporters to keep hold of that enjoyment. For the players it is a short career and I do not blame them for trying to earn as much as possible to safeguard their future after they have hung up their boots. Money, however, should not be the be-all and end-all of everything. I believe that there are too many outside interests and, as a result, the actual game of football is in danger of becoming a secondary interest.

There is still a lot of unemployment in Britain and most fans have to be careful with their money so that they can go each week to watch their heroes. It is up to those heroes to give 100 per cent in order to repay the dedication of their fans. If they are spending too much time on outside interests how can they be so fully focussed, and keen to entertain on a match-day?

I have made quite a number of observations and, yes of course, it is very easy to criticise. So just how do we overcome these problems that I see? Let me give a few suggestions.

Crewe Alexandra in the English Football League is a good example of how it can work. Dario Gradi has been their manager since June 1983. They average just under 4,000 a game, but one thing that you can guarantee is that, when you go to see them play, you will be given good, value-for-money, entertaining football. Winning trophies comes second and the football comes first — and there is also the added bonus of seeing excellent young talent being helped along. They are fearful of nobody and have a lot of fun when they are drawn against a top club in a cup game.

When Jimmy Nicholl, in charge of Raith Rovers,

achieved the same sort of thing. He did not take his side to Ibrox with the sole intention of trying to stop Rangers scoring goals. You cannot prevent top-class players like that from scoring — but you can score enough yourself to get a result and, if all else fails, you can play some real football by which to be remembered. Raith Rovers gained a lot of friends by refusing to shut up shop by sending out a team of robots. There are lessons to be learned by other managers. Be brave! Don't let yourself be pressured by the instant results brigade. Send your team out to play football the way it should be played. Earn the plaudits and the trophies will be sure to follow.

Another suggestion is that much more effort should be made to teach the kids the right way to play by using the talents of those who really know. By that, I am not talking about some nonentity with a badge or a certificate. I am talking about the very people who have been featured in this book. When you go to the VIP lounge after an international these days you are hard pushed to recognise anybody. The room is full of nonentities — people who have been to see the match so that they can pass on the 'technicalities' to their young charges. They know what they can do with their coaching manuals.

If you asked people like Jimmy Johnstone, Jim Baxter, Billy McNeill or Bobby Murdoch to go to the schools and training camps to show the kids and tell them how it should be done, they would be delighted. They have all been there and they know what it is like! They love the game and, like myself, they are pained at the way it is going. They would all love to give something back.

When I was a lad I always tried to emulate my heroes. I was thrilled to see them and I was inspired by them. Can you imagine what it would be like now for schoolboys to get a visit from Willie Henderson to let them see his medals and his caps, tell them about his experiences — and then give them some tips on how to do it?

These guys put life into the game when they were playing and they could still put life into it now. They could play a major part in safeguarding the future of Scottish football. Scottish kids are born with natural skill and passion, but it must be fed.

Yesterday's superstars can turn today's hopefuls into tomorrow's heroes!

My heart's in the Highlands, my heart is not here;

My heart's in the Highlands a-chasing the deer,

Chasing the wild deer, and following the roe,

My heart's in the Highlands, wherever I go.

Rabbie Burns

Index

251

INDEX